SCIENCE FUSION

Assessment Guide

Module A

HOLT McDOUGAL

HOUGHTON MIFFLIN HARCOURT

Acknowledgements for Covers

Cover Photo Credits

DNA molecule (bg) ©Carl Goodman/Meese Photo Research; *false color X-rays on hand* (l) ©Lester Lefkowitz/Getty Images; *primate* (cl) ©Bruno Morandi/The Image Bank/Getty Images; *red cells* (cr) ©Todd Davidson/Getty Images; *fossils* (r) ©Yoshihi Tanaka/amana images/Getty Images

Printed in the U.S.A.

ISBN 978-0-547-59332-6

7 8 9 10 2266 19 18 17 16 15
4500548544   A B C D E F G

Contents

INTRODUCTION
Overview

ScienceFusion provides parallel instructional paths for teaching important science content. You may choose to use the print path, the digital path, or a combination of the two. The quizzes, tests, and other resources in this Assessment Guide may be used with either path.

The *ScienceFusion* assessment options are intended to give you maximum flexibility in assessing what your students know and what they can do. The program's formative and summative assessment categories reflect the understanding that assessment is a learning opportunity for students, and that students must periodically demonstrate mastery of content in cumulative tests.

All *ScienceFusion* tests are available—and editable—in ExamView and online at thinkcentral.com. You can customize a quiz or test for your classroom in many ways:

- adding or deleting items
- adjusting for cognitive complexity, Bloom's taxonomy level, or other measures of difficulty
- changing the sequence of items
- changing the item formats
- editing the question itself

All of these changes, except the last, can be made without invalidating the content correlation of the item.

This Assessment Guide is your directory to assessment in *ScienceFusion*. In it you'll find copymasters for Lesson Quizzes, Unit Tests, Unit Reviews, Performance-Based Assessments Alternative Assessments, and End-of-Module Tests; answers and explanations of answers; rubrics; a bubble-style answer sheet; and suggestions for assessing student progress using performance, portfolio, and other forms of integrated assessment.

You will also find additional assessment prompts and ideas throughout the program, as indicated on the chart that follows.

Assessment in *ScienceFusion* Program

	Student Editions	Teacher Edition	Assessment Guide	Digital Lessons	Online Resources at thinkcental.com	ExamView Test Generator
Formative Assessment						
Assessing Prior Knowledge						
Engage Your Brain	X					
Unit Pretest			X		X	X
Embedded Assessment						
Active Reading Questions	X					
Interactivities	X					
Probing Questions		X				
Formative Assessment		X				
Classroom Discussions		X				
Common Misconceptions		X				
Learning Alerts		X				
Embedded Questions and Tasks				X		
Student Self-Assessments				X		
Digital Lesson Quiz				X		
When used primarily for teaching						
Lesson Review	X	X				
Lesson Quiz			X		X	X
Alternative Assessment			X		X	
Performance-Based Assessment			X			
Portfolio Assessment, guidelines			X			
Summative Assessment						
End of Lessons						
Visual Summary	X	X				
Lesson Quiz			X		X	X
Alternative Assessment		X	X		X	
Rubrics			X		X	
End of Units						
Unit Review	X		X		X	X
Answers		X	X		X	
Test Doctor Answer Explanations		X	X			X
Unit Test A (on level)			X		X	X
Unit Test B (below level)			X		X	X
End of Module						
End-of-Module Test			X		X	X

Formative Assessment
Assessing Prior Knowledge

Frequently in this program, you'll find suggestions for assessing what your students already know before they begin studying a new lesson. These activities help you warm up the class, focus minds, and activate students' prior knowledge.

In This Assessment Guide

Each of the units begins with a Unit Pretest consisting of multiple-choice questions that assess prior and prerequisite knowledge. Use the Pretest to get a snapshot of the class and help you organize your pre-teaching.

In the Student Edition

Engage Your Brain Simple, interactive warm-up tasks get students thinking, and remind them of what they may already know about the lesson topics.

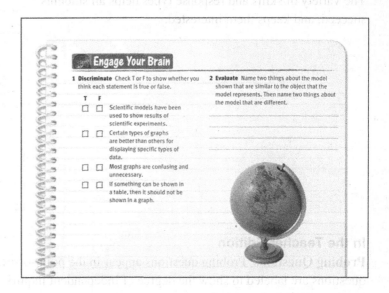

Active Reading Questions Students first see the lesson vocabulary on the opening page, where they are challenged to show what they know about the terms. Multiple exposures to the key terms throughout the lesson lead to mastery.

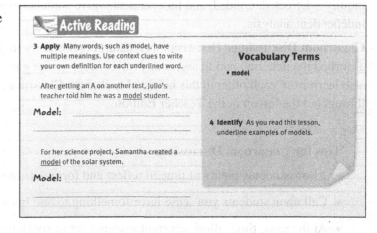

In the Teacher Edition

Opening Your Lesson At the start of each TE lesson Opening Your Lesson suggests questions and activities that help you assess prerequisite and prior knowledge.

Embedded Assessment

Once you're into the lesson, you'll continue to find suggestions, prompts, and resources for ongoing assessment.

Student Edition

Active Reading Questions and Interactivities Frequent questions and interactive prompts are embedded in the text, where they give students instant feedback on their comprehension. They ask students to respond in different ways, such as writing, drawing, and annotating the text. The variety of skills and response types helps all students succeed, and keeps them interested.

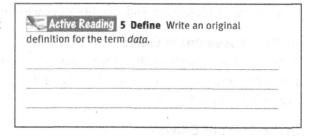

In the Teacher Edition

Probing Questions Probing questions appear in the point-of-use teaching suggestions. These questions are labeled to show the degree of independent inquiry they require. The three levels of inquiry—Directed, Guided, and Independent—give students experience that builds toward independent analysis.

Classroom Discussions Discussion is a natural opportunity to gauge how well students have absorbed the material, and to assess any misconceptions or gaps in their understanding. Students also learn from each other in this informal exchange. Classroom discussion ideas appear throughout the lesson in the Teacher Edition.

Tips for Classroom Discussions

- Allow students plenty of time to reflect and formulate their answers.

- Call upon students you sense have something to add but who haven't spoken.

- At the same time, allow reluctant students not to speak unless they choose to.

- Encourage students to respond to each other as well as to you.

Misconceptions and Learning Alerts The Teacher Background pages at the start of a unit describe common misconceptions and identify the lessons in which the misconceptions can be addressed. Strategies for addressing the misconceptions appear in the point-of-use teaching notes. Additional Learning Alerts help you introduce and assess challenging topics.

Formative Assessment A final formative assessment strategy appears on the Evaluate page at the end of each lesson, followed by reteaching ideas.

In This Assessment Guide

Several of the assessment strategies described in this book can be used either as formative or as summative instruments, depending on whether you use them primarily for teaching or primarily for evaluation. The choice is yours. Among these are the Lesson Quizzes, described here, and the Alternative Assessment, described under Summative Assessment, next. Because both of these assessments are provided for every lesson, you could use them both at different times.

Lesson Quizzes as Formative Assessment In this book, Lesson Quizzes in a unit follow the Unit Pretest. The five-item Lesson Quiz can be administered as a written test, used as an oral quiz, or given to small student groups for collaboration. In the Answer Key at the end of this book, you'll find a feature called the Test Doctor, which provides a brief explanation of what makes each correct answer correct and each incorrect answer incorrect. Use this explanatory material to begin a discussion following the quiz.

Classroom Observation

Classroom observation is one way to gather and record information that can lead to improved instruction. You'll find a Classroom Observation Checklist in Assessment Tools, following the Introduction.

Tips for Classroom Observation

- Don't try to see and record everything at once. Instead, identify specific skills you will observe in a session.

- Don't try to observe everyone at once. Focus on a few students at a time.

- Repeat observations at different times in order to identify patterns. This practice helps you validate or correct your impressions from a single time.

- Use the checklist as is or modify it to suit your students and your instruction. Fill in student names across the top and write the date next to the skills you are observing on a particular day.

- Keep the checklist, add to it, and consult it periodically for hints about strengths, weaknesses, and developments of particular students and of the class.

- Use your own system of ratings or the simple number code on the checklist. When you have not seen enough to give a rating, leave the space blank.

Summative Assessment

In the Student Edition
Visual Summary and Lesson Review
Interactive summaries help students synthesize lesson material, and the Lesson Review provides a variety of questions focusing on vocabulary, key concepts, and critical thinking.

Unit Reviews
Each unit in the Student Edition is followed by a Unit Review, also available in this Assessment Guide. These tests include the item types commonly found on the statewide assessments. You may want to use these tests to review unit content right away or at any time later in the year to help students prepare for the statewide assessment. If you wish to give students practice in filling in a machine-scorable answer sheet, use the bubble-type answer sheet at the start of the Answer Key.

In This Assessment Guide
Alternative Assessments
Every lesson has an Alternative Assessment worksheet, which is previewed in the Teacher Edition on the Evaluate page of the lesson. The activities on these worksheets assess student comprehension of core content, while at the same time offering a variety of options for students with various abilities, learning styles, and interests. The activities require students to produce a tangible product or to give a presentation that demonstrates their understanding of skills and concepts.

Tips for Alternative Assessment

- The structure of these worksheets allows for differentiation in topic, difficulty level, and activity type/learner preferences.

- Each worksheet has a variety of items for students and teachers to choose from.

- The items may relate to the entire lesson content or to just one or two key topics. Encourage students to select items so that they will hit most key topics in a lesson.

- Share the rubrics and Presentation Guidelines with students so they understand the expectations for these assignments. You could have them fill in a rubric with their name and activity choices at the same time they choose their assignments, and then submit the rubric with their presentation or assignment.

Grading Alternative Assessments

Each type of Alternative Assessment worksheet has a rubric for easy grading.

- The rubrics focus mostly on content comprehension, but also take into account presentation.

- The Answer Key describes the expected content mastery for each Alternative Assessment.

- Separate Presentation Guidelines describe the attributes of successful written work, posters and displays, oral presentations, and multimedia presentations.

- Each rubric has space to record your reasons for deducting points, such as content errors or particular presentation flaws.

- If you wish to change the focus of an Alternative Assessment worksheet, you can adjust the point values for the rubric.

The Presentation Guidelines and the rubrics follow the Introduction. The Answer Key appears at the end of the book.

Unit Tests A and B

This Assessment Guide contains leveled tests for each unit.

- The A-level tests are for students who typically perform below grade level.

- The B-level tests are intended for students whose performance is on grade level.

Both versions of the test address the unit content with a mixture of item types, including multiple choice, short response, and extended response. Both levels contains items of low, medium, and high cognitive complexity, though level B contains more items of higher complexity. A few items appear in both of the tests as a means of assuring parallel content coverage. If you need a higher-level test, you can easily assemble one from the lesson assessment banks in ExamView or online at thinkcentral.com. All items in the banks are tagged with five different measures of difficulty as well as standards and key terms.

End-of-Module Test

The final test in this Assessment Guide is the End-of-Module Review. This is a long-form, multiple-choice test in the style of the statewide assessments. An Answer Sheet appears with the review.

Performance-Based Assessment

Performance-Based Assessment involves a hands-on activity in which students demonstrate their skills and thought processes. Each Performance-Based Assessment includes a page of teacher-focused information and a general rubric for scoring. In addition to the Performance-Based Assessment provided for each unit, you can use many of the labs in the program as the basis for performance assessment.

Tips for Performance Assessment

- Prepare materials and stations so that all students have the same tasks. You may want to administer performance assessments to different groups over time.

- Provide clear expectations, including the measures on which students will be evaluated. You may invite them to help you formulate or modify the rubric.

- Assist students as needed, but avoid supplying answers to those who can handle the work on their own.

- Don't be hurried. Allow students enough time to do their best work.

Developing or Modifying a Rubric

Developing a rubric for a performance task involves three basic steps:

1. Identify the inquiry skills that are taught in the lesson and that students must perform to complete the task successfully and identify the understanding of content that is also required. Many of the skills may be found in the Lab and Activity Evaluation later in this guide.

2. Determine which skills and understandings of content are involved in each step.

3. Decide what you will look for to confirm that the student has acquired each skill and understanding you identified.

Portfolio Assessment, Guidelines

A portfolio is a showcase for student work, a place where many types of assignments, projects, reports and data sheets can be collected. The work samples in the collection provide snapshots of the student's efforts over time, and taken together they reveal the student's growth, attitudes, and understanding better than other types of assessment. Portfolio assessment involves meeting with each student to discuss the work and to set goals for future performance. In contrast with formal assessments, portfolio assessments have these advantages:

1. They give students a voice in the assessment process.
2. They foster reflection, self-monitoring, and self-evaluation.
3. They provide a comprehensive picture of a student's progress.

Tips for Portfolio Assessment

- Make a basic plan. Decide how many work samples will be included in the portfolios and what period of time they represent.

- Explain the portfolio and its use. Describe the portfolio an artist might put together, showing his or her best or most representative work, as part of an application for school or a job. The student's portfolio is based on this model.

- Together with your class decide on the required work samples that everyone's portfolio will contain.

- Explain that the students will choose additional samples of their work to include. Have students remember how their skills and understanding have grown over the period covered by the portfolio, and review their work with this in mind. The best pieces to choose may not be the longest or neatest.

- Give students the Portfolio Planning Worksheet found in Assessment Tools. Have students record their reasoning as they make their selections and assemble their portfolios.

- Share with students the Portfolio Evaluation Checklist, also found in Assessment Tools, and explain how you will evaluate the contents of their portfolios.

- Use the portfolios for conferences, grading, and planning. Give students the option of taking their portfolios home to share.

ASSESSMENT TOOLS
Alternative Assessment Presentation Guidelines

The following guidelines can be used as a starting point for evaluating student presentation of alternative assessments. For each category, use only the criteria that are relevant for the particular format you are evaluating; some criteria will not apply for certain formats.

Written Work

- Matches the assignment in format (essay, journal entry, newspaper report, etc.)
- Begins with a clear statement of the topic and purpose
- Provides information that is essential to the reader's understanding
- Supporting details are precise, related to the topic, and effective
- Follows a logical pattern of organization
- Uses transitions between ideas
- When appropriate, uses diagrams or other visuals
- Correct spelling, capitalization, and punctuation
- Correct grammar and usage
- Varied sentence structures
- Neat and legible

Posters and Displays

- Matches the assignment in format (brochure, poster, storyboard, etc.)
- Topic is well researched and quality information is presented
- Poster communicates an obvious, overall message
- Posters have large titles and the message, or purpose, is obvious
- Images are big, clear, and convey important information
- More important ideas and items are given more space and presented with larger images or text
- Colors are used for a purpose, such as to link words and images
- Sequence of presentation is easy to follow because of visual cues, such as arrows, letters, or numbers
- Artistic elements are appropriate and add to the overall presentation
- Text is neat
- Captions and labels have correct spelling, capitalization, and punctuation

Oral Presentations

- Matches the assignment in format (speech, news report, etc.)
- Presentation is delivered well, and enthusiasm is shown for topic
- Words are clearly pronounced and can easily be heard
- Information is presented in a logical, interesting sequence that the audience can follow
- Visual aids are relative to content, very neat, and artistic
- Often makes eye contact with audience
- Listens carefully to questions from the audience and responds accurately
- Stands straight, facing the audience
- Uses movements appropriate to the presentation; does not fidget
- Covers the topic well in the time allowed
- Gives enough information to clarify the topic, but does not include irrelevant details

Multimedia Presentations

- Topic is well researched, and essential information is presented
- The product shows evidence of an original and inventive approach
- The presentation conveys an obvious, overall message
- Contains all the required media elements, such as text, graphics, sounds, videos, and animations
- Fonts and formatting are used appropriately to emphasize words; color is used appropriately to enhance the fonts
- Sequence of presentation is logical and/or the navigation is easy and understandable
- Artistic elements are appropriate and add to the overall presentation
- The combination of multimedia elements with words and ideas produces an effective presentation
- Written elements have correct spelling, capitalization, and punctuation

Alternative Assessment Rubric – Tic-Tac-Toe

Worksheet Title: _____

Student Name: _____

Date: _____

Add the titles of each activity chosen to the chart below.

	Content *(0-3 points)*	**Presentation** *(0-2 points)*	***Points*** ***Sum***
Choice 1: _____			
Points			
Reason for missing points			
Choice 2: _____			
Points			
Reason for missing points			
Choice 3: _____			
Points			
Reason for missing points			
		Total Points (of 15 maximum)	

Alternative Assessment Rubric – Mix and Match

Worksheet Title: _____

Student Name: _____

Date: _____

Add the column choices to the chart below.

	Content *(0-3 points)*	**Presentation** *(0-2 points)*	**Points Sum**
Information Source from Column A: _____ Topics Chosen for Column B: _____ _____ Presentation Format from Column C: _____			
Points			
Reason for missing points			
		Total Points (of 5 maximum)	

Alternative Assessment Rubric – Take Your Pick

Worksheet Title: _____

Student Name: _____

Date: _____

Add the titles of each activity chosen to the chart below.

2-point item: 5-point item 8-point item:	**Content** *(0-1.5 points)* *(0-4 points)* *(0-6 points)*	**Presentation** *(0-0.5 point)* *(0-1 point)* *(0-2 points)*	***Points*** ***Sum***
Choice 1: _____			
Points			
Reason for missing points			
Choice 2: _____			
Points			
Reason for missing points			
		Total Points (of 10 maximum)	

Alternative Assessment Rubric – Choose Your Meal

Worksheet Title: _____

Student Name: _____

Date: _____

Add the titles of each activity chosen to the chart below.

Appetizer, side dish, or dessert: Main Dish	**Content** *(0-3 points)* *(0-6 points)*	**Presentation** *(0-2) points* *(0-4 points)*	*Points Sum*
Appetizer: _____			
Points			
Reason for missing points			
Side Dish: _____			
Points			
Reason for missing points			
Main Dish: _____			
Points			
Reason for missing points			
Dessert: _____			
Points			
Reason for missing points			
		Total Points (of 25 maximum)	

Alternative Assessment Rubric – Points of View

Worksheet Title: _____

Student Name: _____

Date: _____

Add the titles of group's assignment to the chart below.

	Content (0-4 points)	Presentation (0-1 points)	Points Sum
Point of View:			
Points			
Reason for missing points			
		Total Points (of 5 maximum)	

Alternative Assessment Rubric – Climb the Pyramid

Worksheet Title: _____

Student Name: _____

Date: _____

Add the titles of each activity chosen to the chart below.

	Content (0-3 points)	**Presentation** (0-2 points)	*Points Sum*
Choice from bottom row: _____			
Points			
Reason for missing points			
Choice from middle row: _____			
Points			
Reason for missing points			
Top row: _____			
Points			
Reason for missing points			
		Total Points (of 15 maximum)	

Alternative Assessment Rubric – Climb the Ladder

Worksheet Title: _____

Student Name: _____

Date: _____

Add the titles of each activity chosen to the chart below.

	Content (0-3 points)	Presentation (0-2 points)	Points Sum
Choice 1 (top rung): _____			
Points			
Reason for missing points			
Choice 2 (middle rung): _____			
Points			
Reason for missing points			
Choice 3 (bottom rung): _____			
Points			
Reason for missing points			
		Total Points (of 15 maximum)	

Date _____

Rating Scale			
3	Outstanding	1	Needs Improvement
2	Satisfactory		Not Enough Opportunity to Observe

Names of Students

Inquiry Skills										
Observe										
Compare										
Classify/Order										
Gather, Record, Display, or Interpret Data										
Use Numbers										
Communicate										
Plan and Conduct Simple Investigations										
Measure										
Predict										
Infer										
Draw Conclusions										
Use Time/Space Relationships										
Hypothesize										
Formulate or Use Models										
Identify and Control Variables										
Experiment										

Lab and Activity Evaluation

Circle the appropriate number for each criterion. Then add up the circled numbers in each column and record the sum in the subtotals row at the bottom. Add up these subtotals to get the total score.

Graded by _____ Total _____ /100

Behavior	Completely	Mostly	Partially	Poorly
Follows lab procedures carefully and fully	10–9	8–7–6	5–4–3	2–1–0
Wears the required safety equipment and displays knowledge of safety procedures and hazards	10–9	8–7–6	5–4–3	2–1–0
Uses laboratory time productively and stays on task	10–9	8–7–6	5–4–3	2–1–0
Behavior	**Completely**	**Mostly**	**Partially**	**Poorly**
Uses tools, equipment, and materials properly	10–9	8–7–6	5–4–3	2–1–0
Makes quantitative observations carefully, with precision and accuracy	10–9	8–7–6	5–4–3	2–1–0
Uses the appropriate SI units to collect quantitative data	10–9	8–7–6	5–4–3	2–1–0
Records accurate qualitative data during the investigation	10–9	8–7–6	5–4–3	2–1–0
Records measurements and observations in clearly organized tables that have appropriate headings and units	10–9	8–7–6	5–4–3	2–1–0
Works well with partners	10–9	8–7–6	5–4–3	2–1–0
Efficiently and properly solves any minor problems that might occur with materials or procedures	10–9	8–7–6	5–4–3	2–1–0
Subtotals:				

Comments

_____

_____

_____

_____

My Science Portfolio

What Is in My Portfolio	Why I Chose It
1.	
2.	
3.	
4.	
5.	
6.	
7.	

I organized my Science Portfolio this way because _____

_____

_____

_____

_____

Name _____ Date _____

Portfolio Evaluation Checklist

Aspects of Science Literacy	Evidence of Growth
1. Understands science concepts *(Animals, Plants; Earth's Land, Air, Water; Space; Weather; Matter, Motion, Energy)*	_____ _____ _____
2. Uses inquiry skills *(observes, compares, classifies, gathers/ interprets data, communicates, measures, experiments, infers, predicts, draws conclusions)*	_____ _____ _____
3. Thinks critically *(analyzes, synthesizes, evaluates, applies ideas effectively, solves problems)*	_____ _____ _____
4. Displays traits/attitudes of a scientist *(is curious, questioning, persistent, precise, creative, enthusiastic; uses science materials carefully; is concerned for environment)*	_____ _____ _____

Summary of Portfolio Assessment

For This Review			Since Last Review		
Excellent	Good	Fair	Improving	About the Same	Not as Good

Cells

Choose the letter of the best answer.

1. Which of the following is a plant organ responsible for trapping light energy to make food?

   A. leaf

   B. fruit

   C. petal

   D. root

2. The following picture shows a microscopic view of blood. Blood is made of different types of cells that work together.

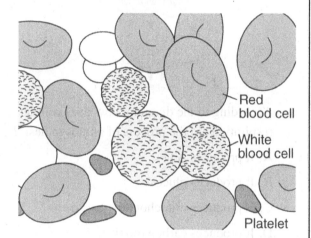

   Which of the following best describes blood?

   A. organ

   B. tissue

   C. organism

   D. organ system

3. In biology class, Zach observes cells. Each cell has a structure that separates the inside of the cell from the environment. Which structure is Zach observing?

   A. nucleus

   B. cytoskeleton

   C. cell membrane

   D. genetic material

4. Which of these is the smallest?

   A. cells

   B. atoms

   C. molecules

   D. cell membranes

5. What is the result of homeostasis at the cellular level?

   A. The cell dies.

   B. The cell divides.

   C. The cell no longer obtains energy.

   D. The environment within the cell is stable.

6. Which of the following describes the structure of the endoplasmic reticulum?

   A. a system of folded membranes

   B. a tiny organelle that has no membrane

   C. a rigid, protective layer found outside the cell membrane

   D. an organelle surrounded by a double membrane and containing DNA

7. The diagram below shows molecules inside and outside of a cell. Molecules move from areas of high concentration to low concentration.

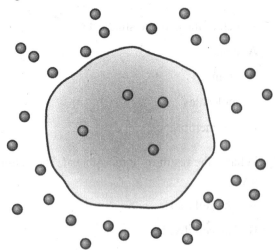

What is the name of the process that will move molecules into the cell?

A. diffusion

B. exocytosis

C. photosynthesis

D. cellular respiration

8. Which of the following statements describes a characteristic of a eukaryote?

A. It has no cytoplasm.

B. It has DNA in a nucleus.

C. It is made of many cells.

D. It has DNA in its cytoplasm.

9. Plants can provide the materials that animals use in cellular respiration, and animals can provide some of the materials that plants use for photosynthesis. This image below shows the relationship between photosynthesis and cellular respiration.

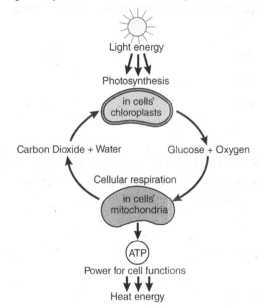

According to the diagram, how does cellular respiration aid the process of photosynthesis?

A. It produces ATP.

B. It produces glucose.

C. It produces mitochondria.

D. It produces carbon dioxide.

10. Nutritionists know that lipids are a vital nutrient that helps keep cells working properly. What is one way the cells in our bodies use lipids?

A. to make amino acids

B. to repair broken bones

C. to form cell membranes

D. to carry information in the cell

The Characteristics of Cells

Choose the letter of the best answer.

1. What term describes the smallest unit that can perform all of the functions necessary for life?

   A. a single cell

   B. a cell nucleus

   C. a cell membrane

   D. a multicellular organism

2. Eukaryotic cells and prokaryotic cells have some parts in common. Which of the following pairs of parts would you find in **both** types of cells?

   A. cytoplasm and nucleus

   B. cell membrane and cytoplasm

   C. DNA and membrane-bound organelles

   D. cell membrane and membrane-bound organelles

3. According to Theodor Schwann, all parts of organisms are made up of which of the following?

   A. cells

   B. nuclei

   C. organs

   D. organelles

4. Robert Hooke was the first person to describe cells. Which of the following instruments did he use to make his observations?

   A.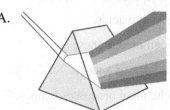

   B.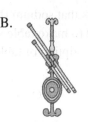

   C.

   D.

5. What did Robert Virchow observe about cell division?

   A. Cells have nuclei.

   B. Cells move around.

   C. Cells have cell membranes.

   D. Cells come from other cells.

Chemistry of Life

Choose the letter of the best answer.

1. Some dog foods contain corn and wheat that provide the dog with carbohydrates. Why are carbohydrates important to cell processes?

   A. They make amino acids.

   B. They form cell membranes.

   C. They are a source of energy.

   D. They help chemical processes happen.

2. Ms. Salis explains to her class that sodium (Na) and chlorine (Cl) atoms bond to make table salt (NaCl). Which is the **best** description of table salt?

   A. It is a cell.

   B. It is an atom.

   C. It is an element.

   D. It is a compound.

3. Which of these is one of the six **most** common elements found in the human body?

   A. iron

   B. helium

   C. oxygen

   D. water

4. Alejandro is doing a science experiment. He is given a substance made up of one of the four main types of molecules found in the cells of living things. He notices that the substance does not mix with water.

   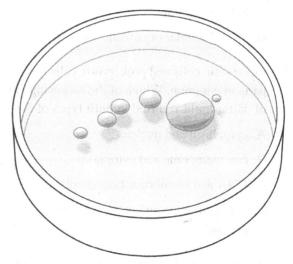

   Based on the fact that it does **not** mix with water, what can Alejandro conclude about the molecule?

   A. It is a lipid.

   B. It is a protein.

   C. It is a nucleic acid.

   D. It is a carbohydrate.

5. DNA stores genetic information. What type of molecule is DNA?

   A. lipid

   B. protein

   C. nucleic acid

   D. carbohydrate

Cell Structure and Function

Choose the letter of the best answer.

1. Under a high-powered microscope, Dan sees a cellular organelle. The organelle has a double membrane, and the inner membrane is folded. The organelle contains its own DNA. Which organelle does Dan see?

   A. endoplasmic reticulum

   B. mitochondrion

   C. nucleus

   D. ribosome

2. In what way could two eukaryotic cells be different from each other?

   A. One eukaryotic cell could have cytoplasm while another does not.

   B. One eukaryotic cell could have a cell membrane while another does not.

   C. Two eukaryotic cells could differ in the number and types of organelles they contain.

   D. Two eukaryotic cells could differ in the number and types of prokaryotes they contain.

3. Which of the following describes the cytoskeleton?

   A. a web of proteins that gives shape and support to the cell

   B. a membrane-bound organelle that contains genetic material

   C. the outer covering of a cell that separates it from the environment

   D. the structure that contains the information about how to make a cell's proteins

4. What is the main function of chloroplasts in a plant cell?

   A. They produce proteins.

   B. They store water and food.

   C. They perform photosynthesis.

   D. They protect cells from the surrounding environment.

5. Jun Ming puts a slide of a eukaryotic cell under a microscope. The following diagram represents what Jun Ming observes.

   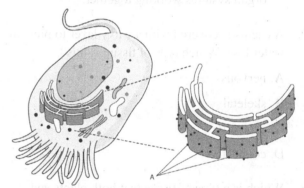

   Which of the following choices **best** describes the structures labeled A?

   A. These structures do not have membranes.

   B. These structures transport substances throughout the cell.

   C. These structures produce energy for the cell in the form of ATP.

   D. These structures contain DNA and have a folded inner membrane.

Name _____ Date _____

Levels of Cellular Organization

Choose the letter of the best answer.

1. Which statement best explains the relationship between structure and function in an organism?

   A. Structure and function refer to the different tissue types within an organism.

   B. Structure and function refer to the jobs of tissues, organs, and organ systems.

   C. Structure and function refer to the locations of tissues, organs, and organ systems.

   D. Structure and function refer to the locations and jobs of different tissues, organs, and organ systems working together.

2. A cactus is covered with a waxy layer to prevent water loss. Which type of tissue is this?

   A. nervous

   B. skeletal

   C. protective

   D. connective

3. Which is a type of tissue that both plants and animals have?

   A. nerve

   B. ground

   C. protective

   D. connective

4. The diagram shows parts of the human body. These parts work together to help you digest the food you eat.

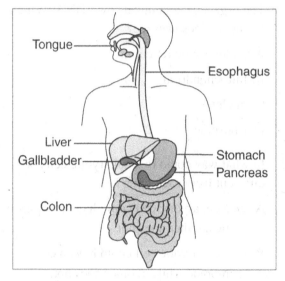

   Which term describes the stomach?

   A. cell

   B. organ

   C. tissue

   D. organ system

5. Eugene is studying the levels of structural organization of an animal's body. Which level would describe a dog's eye?

   A. organ

   B. tissue

   C. organism

   D. organ system

Homeostasis and Cell Processes

Choose the letter of the best answer.

1. In one type of cell division, a single cell forms two new cells. This process is called mitosis. What is a reason that human skin cells frequently undergo mitosis?

   A. to get energy for the body

   B. to prevent bruises on the body

   C. to replace dead or damaged skin cells

   D. to replace dead or damaged muscle cells

2. Cells must be able to perform certain functions in order to survive. Which of the following must all cells do to survive?

   A. obtain energy

   B. absorb wastes

   C. utilize oxygen

   D. continue growing

3. Organisms can respond to changes in their environment in order to maintain a balance, called homeostasis. What does a tree do to maintain homeostasis during the winter months?

   A. shivers

   B. hibernates

   C. absorbs sun

   D. loses leaves

4. Molecules move in and out of a cell by diffusion. The picture shows a cell and molecules both inside and outside the cell.

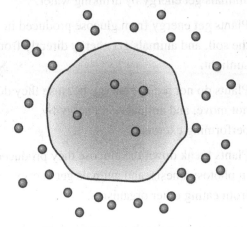

   How will the molecules in this illustration move as a result of diffusion?

   A. into the cell

   B. out of the cell

   C. into another cell

   D. to the external environment

5. Homeostasis is necessary for a cell to survive. What is the definition of homeostasis?

   A. the elimination of wastes

   B. the division of cells to form new cells

   C. the maintenance of a stable internal environment

   D. the process by which energy from the sun is used to make food

Photosynthesis and Cellular Respiration

Lesson Quiz

Choose the letter of the best answer.

1. How do organisms get the energy they need?

    A. Plants get energy from fertilizers, and animals get energy by drinking water.

    B. Plants get energy from glucose produced in the soil, and animals get energy directly from sunlight.

    C. Plants do not require energy because they do not move, and animals get energy by performing exercise.

    D. Plants break down the glucose they produced in photosynthesis, and animals get energy from eating other organisms.

2. Green plants produce their own food during photosynthesis. Which of these statements about photosynthesis is true?

    A. Water is one product of photosynthesis.

    B. Oxygen is one product of photosynthesis.

    C. Chlorophyll is one product of photosynthesis.

    D. Carbon dioxide is one product of photosynthesis.

3. What is the food that plants produce during photosynthesis?

    A. glucose

    B. chlorophyll

    C. chloroplasts

    D. carbon dioxide

4. There is a connection between photosynthesis and cellular respiration. The products from one provide the raw materials for the other. This image shows the relationship between the two processes.

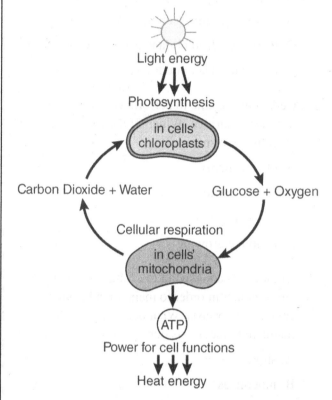

What products of photosynthesis are starting material for cellular respiration?

    A. glucose and oxygen

    B. heat energy and ATP

    C. carbon dioxide and water

    D. light energy and chlorophyll

5. What do animals do with the carbon dioxide produced in their cells during cellular respiration?

    A. store it for later use

    B. reuse it during photosynthesis

    C. exhale it in the breathing process

    D. combine it with water to make sugar

The Characteristics of Cells

Tic-Tac-Toe: *The Basic Unit of Life*

1. Work on your own, with a partner, or with a small group.

2. Choose three quick activities from the game. Check the boxes you plan to complete. They must form a straight line in any direction.

3. Have your teacher approve your plan.

4. Do each activity, and turn in your results.

__ **Historical Cell Fiction**	__ **Something in Common**	__ **A Great Adventure**
Research information on the scientists who contributed to the cell theory. Then, write a fictional story in which the scientists meet and discuss their ideas about cells.	Make a drawing of a eukaryotic cell and label its major parts. Make a drawing of a prokaryotic cell and label its major parts. Place the drawings side by side and use string or yarn to connect the common parts.	Pretend you are running an amusement park. All of the rides are built to resemble structures found within a eukaryotic cell. Write a guidebook describing each ride and what it does. Include a color-coded map of the amusement park.
__ **A Simple Cell**	__ **How It Works**	__ **Time Capsule**
Write a poem about being a prokaryotic cell. Select a type of bacteria or archaea. Include facts about this organism in the poem.	Write a persuasive essay about why it is a good thing to be small. Include information about why a cell must be small, and why it cannot survive if it is too large.	Write a journal entry from the point of view of Theodor Schwann. Describe his conclusions about cells.
__ **A Model of a Cell**	__ **Public Service Announcement**	__ **A New Report**
Make a 3-dimensional model of a eukaryotic cell using art supplies. Each organelle must be labeled and be a different color. Include a key that identifies each organelle.	Create an advertising campaign to tell people about the importance of the cell theory. Include a drawing to help convey your message.	Write a news report about a single-celled organism that lives inside your body. Include what this organism is, what it does, and where it can be found.

Name _____ Date _____

Chemistry of Life

Points of View: *Exploring Atoms and Molecules*
**Your class will work together to show what you've learned
about the building blocks of organisms.**

1. Work in groups as assigned by your teacher. Each group will be assigned to one or two viewpoints.

2. Complete your assignment, and present your perspective to the class.

Vocabulary In your own words, define the terms *compound*, *nutrient*, *protein*, and *element*. Then write down a dictionary or textbook definition. Use each term in a sentence that describes how it relates to the cell.

Details Describe how sugars and starches are related to carbohydrates. Then describe how amino acids are related to proteins. Finally, describe how DNA and nucleotides are related to nucleic acids.

Illustrations Draw models of an atom and a water molecule. Finally, draw an illustration depicting how atoms and molecules relate to cells.

Analysis Create a diagram that explains how the terms *molecule*, *atom*, *element*, and *compound* relate to each other.

Models Find a way to model the cell membrane. Make sure your model shows how the phospholipid molecules form this membrane.

Cell Structure and Function

Mix and Match: *Structure and Function of Cell Organelles*
Mix and match ideas to show what you've learned about the structure and function of cells.

1. Work on your own, with a partner, or with a small group.

2. Choose one information source from Column A, two topics from Column B, and one option from Column C. Check your choices.

3. Have your teacher approve your plan.

4. Submit or present your results.

A. Choose One Information Source	B. Choose Two Things to Analyze	C. Choose One Way to Communicate Analysis
___ observations of cells with a microscope ___ photographs of prokaryotic and eukaryotic cells ___ photographs of cell organelles ___ illustrations of cells and the types of organelles ___ video that includes the structure and function of various cell organelles engaged in life processes ___ print or audio description that includes the life processes of a cell ___ digital simulation of cell organelles and their life processes	___ the difference between prokaryotes and eukaryotes ___ the general characteristics of the eukaryotic cell ___ how mitochondria function ___ how the ribosomes, ER, and the Golgi complex work together ___ Differences and similarities between the cell wall and the large central vacuole of plants ___ the differences between chloroplasts found in plant cells and the lysosomes found in animal cells	___ diagram or illustration ___ colors, symbols, and/or arrows marked on a visual, with a key ___ model, such as drawings or descriptions showing differences or relationships ___ field guide describing structures found in eukaryotic cells ___ game ___ story, song, or poem, with supporting details ___ skit, chant, or dance, with supporting details ___ multimedia presentation ___ _____

Levels of Cellular Organization

Tic-Tac-Toe: *Design Artificial Organs*

Imagine that you are on a committee that is considering whether or not to create artificial cells, tissues, or organs.

1. Work on your own, with a partner, or with a small group.

2. Choose three quick activities from the game. Check the boxes you plan to complete. They must form a straight line in any direction.

3. Have your teacher approve your plan.

4. Do each activity, and turn in your results.

__ **Structure and Function**	__ **Diagram**	__ **Organ Journal**
Every organ has a structure directly related to its function. Describe two organs and explain how each organ's structure helps it to function. Then, pick one of these organs and describe what type of artificial structure you think would be ideal for its function, and why.	Choose two or more organ systems and draw a diagram showing how they work together keep an organism healthy. You can choose either plant or animal systems.	Write a journal entry describing two artificial organs you would like to create. Include a diagram of these organs.
__ **Human Cell Types**	__ **Building a System**	__ **Instruction Booklet**
Look up different human cell types. There are more than 200! Briefly describe the function of 10 human body cells. Pick one type you would want to create and tell why, or discuss why this type of cell could never be created artificially.	The four levels of organization (cells, tissues, organs, and organ systems) are nearly the same for all multicellular organisms. Write a skit describing how these four levels make up an organism.	Pick an organ system. Research the names of the organs that make up this system. Design an instruction booklet on the use of this system.
__ **Designer Cell**	__ **Life in a Pond**	__ **Which Tissue?**
Design and sketch an imaginary specialized cell that could be part of an artificial life form. Describe the function of this cell that makes it unique.	Write a poem comparing a single-celled paramecium and a multicellular sunfish living in the same freshwater pond. Explore ways in which each organism is adapted for survival.	Describe the functions of the four types of tissues found in humans. Decide which type you think might be the most useful to manufacture, and compose a speech to convince others of the value of this type of tissue.

Homeostasis and Cell Processes

Climb the Ladder: *Maintaining Homeostasis*

Select an idea from each rung of the ladder to show what you've learned about the different ways organisms maintain homeostasis.

1. Work on your own, with a partner, or with a small group.
2. Choose one item from each rung of the ladder. Check your choices.
3. Have your teacher approve your plan.
4. Submit or present your results.

__ **Illustrate a Poster**	__ **Build a Model**
Make a poster illustrating photosynthesis and cellular respiration. You can illustrate the starting materials and end products with drawings or photographs. Include an explanation of why these two processes relate.	Make a 3-D model of photosynthesis and cellular respiration. Use items such as clay, marshmallows, or pipe cleaners to represent the starting materials and end products. Give an oral explanation of why these processes are essential to cells' survival.
__ **Write a Picture Book**	__ **Be a Broadcaster**
Write a picture book that shows the different stages of the eukaryotic cell cycle. Label the nucleus and chromosomes. Write one sentence to explain each stage of the cycle.	Look at the photographs of the plant and animal cell dividing. Imagine that you are a news broadcaster and these photographs are being shown behind you. Describe in detail what is happening as if it were breaking news. You can write or record your broadcast.
__ **Write a Skit**	__ **Create an Animation**
Write a skit that describes passive and active transport. Assign roles to the different type of materials that need to pass through a membrane. Include information on how these methods of transport help cells maintain balance.	Use a computer program to create an animation to demonstrate passive and active transport. Include a spoken description of both types of transport and how these help the cell maintain balance.

Photosynthesis and Cellular Respiration

Points of View: *Energy Flows!*

Your class will work together to show what you've learned about how energy flows from several different viewpoints.

1. Work in groups as assigned by your teacher. Each group will be assigned to one or two viewpoints.

2. Complete your assignment, and present your perspective to the class.

 Vocabulary Define *photosynthesis* and *cellular respiration* in terms of how energy flows. Then write three sentences that use the words to show the sequence of events that occur during photosynthesis and cellular respiration.

 Examples Find two types of plants in your classroom or an outside area. Explain a possible pathway of flow of energy to and from each plant.

 Illustrations Make illustrations to compare photosynthesis with cellular respiration. How are they similar? How are they different? Can you think of an analogy for the relationship between photosynthesis and cellular respiration?

 Analysis Analyze the elements and compounds of photosynthesis and cellular respiration based on their chemical formulas. Make a chart to show how many atoms of each type are in the starting and end products. Then compare the four (the start and end for each of the two equations).

 Modeling Make a clay or other three-dimensional model of the flow of energy that includes photosynthesis and cellular respiration. Use your model to estimate how much photosynthesis is needed relative to a plant's cellular respiration.

Using Venn Diagrams to Compare Cells

Purpose In this activity, students will draw three cells (animal cell, plant cell, and prokaryotic cell) and compare the cells using a Venn diagram.

Time Period 30–45 minutes

Preparation Gather colored pencils and a piece of paper.

Teaching Strategies This activity is ideal for individual students. You may wish to administer this assessment as an open-book activity. Once students have completed their own Venn diagrams, it may be helpful to have the students compare them with each other.

Scoring Rubric

Possible points	Performance indicators
0–10	Appropriate use of materials and equipment
0–60	Quality of drawings and Venn diagram
0–30	Explanation and analysis of diagrams

Using Venn Diagrams to Compare Cells

Objective

In this activity you will draw cells and then compare them using a three-circle Venn diagram.

Know the Score!

As you work through this activity, keep in mind that you will be earning a grade for the following:

- how well you work with the materials (10%)
- how well you draw the cell diagrams and complete the Venn diagram (60%)
- how well you complete the analysis (30%)

Materials and Equipment

- colored pencils

Procedure

1. Draw and label a prokaryotic cell, an animal cell, and a plant cell in the boxes below. Label as many cell parts as you can.

Prokaryotic cell	Animal cell	Plant cell

2. Complete the Venn diagram to show the cell parts and other characteristics of the three cells. Write characteristics and cell parts that the cells share in overlapping portions of the circles. Write characteristics and cell parts that the cells do not share in portions of the circles that do not overlap.

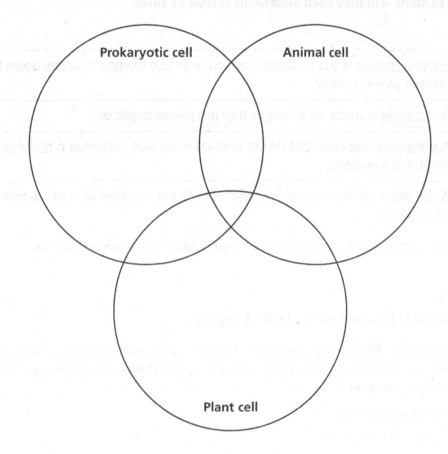

Prokaryotic cell

Animal cell

Plant cell

Analysis

3. In addition to the cell parts, add other characteristics of cells to the Venn diagram.

4. Which two cells are most alike? Explain your answer.

_____

_____

_____

5. Most cells do not look exactly like the diagrams. For example, while most plant cells contain chloroplasts, the cells in the roots of some plants do not. Explain how the parts of a cell (the cell's structure) relate to its function.

_____

_____

_____

_____

Unit 1: Cells

Vocabulary
Check the box to show whether each statement is true or false.

T	F	
☐	☐	1. <u>Photosynthesis</u> is the process in which cells use oxygen to break down food and release stored energy.
☐	☐	2. A <u>molecule</u> is made up of atoms that are joined together.
☐	☐	3. A <u>eukaryote</u> has cells that do not contain a nucleus, whereas a <u>prokaryote</u> has cells that have a nucleus.
☐	☐	4. A cell organelle that is found in animal cells but usually not in plant cells is a <u>lysosome</u>.
☐	☐	5. A <u>tissue</u> is a group of similar cells that perform a common function.

Key Concepts
Read each question below, and circle the best answer.

6. Prem finds an unusual object on the forest floor. After he examines it under a microscope and performs several lab tests, he concludes that the object is a living thing. Which of the following observations most likely led to Prem's conclusion?

    A. The object contained carbon.

    B. Prem saw cells in the object.

    C. The object had a green color.

    D. Prem saw minerals inside the object.

7. Which of the following substances must animal cells take in from the environment to maintain homeostasis?

    A. DNA

    B. oxygen

    C. chlorophyll

    D. carbon dioxide

8. Juana made the following table.

Organelle	Function
Mitochondrion	Cellular respiration
Ribosome	DNA synthesis
Chloroplast	Photosynthesis
Endoplasmic reticulum	Makes proteins and lipids
Golgi complex	Packages proteins

Juana's table lists several cell organelles and their functions, but she made an error. Which of the organelles shown in the table is listed with the wrong function?

A. mitochondrion   C. cell membrane

B. ribosome   D. Golgi complex

9. Which molecule is a source of energy, a store of energy in the body, and can mix with water?

A. lipid   C. nucleic acid

B. chlorophyll   D. carbohydrate

10. Which method of material exchange uses up energy?

A. osmosis   C. active transport

B. diffusion   D. passive transport

11. The following diagram shows a common cell organelle.

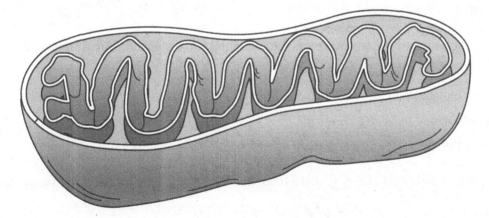

What process takes place in the organelle shown?

A. photosynthesis   C. cellular respiration

B. protein synthesis   D. packaging of proteins

12. Plants contain xylem and phloem tissue. What organ system in animals performs a similar function as the xylem and phloem of plants?

A. digestive system

B. excretory system

C. respiratory system

D. circulatory system

13. Which statement correctly tells why the cells of unicellular and multicellular organisms divide?

A. The cells of unicellular organisms divide to reproduce; those of multicellular organisms divide to replace cells and to grow.

B. The cells of unicellular organisms divide to replace cells and to grow; those of multicellular organisms divide to reproduce.

C. The cells of both kinds of organisms divide to reproduce.

D. The cells of both kinds of organisms divide to replace cells and to grow.

14. The following picture shows *Escherichia coli* cells, a species of bacterium.

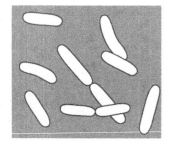

Which of the following statements correctly compares the cells shown in the picture with a human cell?

A. Both types of cells divide by mitosis.

B. Human cells contain proteins but *E. coli* cells do not.

C. Both cells contain ribosomes and a cell membrane.

D. Human cells contain DNA but *E. coli* cells do not.

15. A plant leaf is an organ that traps light energy to make food. In what way is an animal stomach similar to a plant leaf?

A. Both organs make food.

B. Both organs are made up of only one kind of cell.

C. Both organs are made up of several kinds of tissues.

D. Both organs take in oxygen and release carbon dioxide.

16. The following table shows the surface area-to-volume ratio of four cube-shaped cell models.

Cell Model	Surface Area	Volume	Surface Area-to Volume Ratio
A	6 cm^2	1 cm^3	6 : 1 = 6
B	24 cm^2	8 cm^3	24 : 8 = 3
C	54 cm^2	27 cm^3	54 : 27 = 2
D	96 cm^2	64 cm^3	96 : 64 = 1.5

Cells are small, and their surface area is large in relation to their volume. This is an important feature for the proper transport of nutrients and water in to and out of the cell. Which of the four model cells do you think will be best able to supply nutrients and water to its cell parts?

A. cell model A

B. cell model B

C. cell model C

D. cell model D

17. Cells of a multicellular organism are specialized. What does this statement mean?

A. Cells of a multicellular organism are adapted to perform specific functions.

B. Cells of a multicellular organism perform all life functions but not at the same time.

C. Cells of a multicellular organism are specialized because they have a complex structure.

D. Cells of a multicellular organism can perform all the life functions the organism needs to survive.

Critical Thinking
Answer the following questions in the space provided.

18. The following diagram shows a cell that Dimitri saw on his microscope slide.

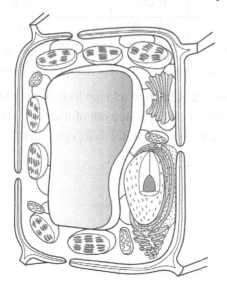

Dimitri's teacher gave him an unlabeled slide of some cells and asked him to identify whether the cells were plant cells or animal cells. Dimitri examined the slide under a microscope and concluded that the cells were plant cells. How did Dimitri reach his conclusion? Is his conclusion correct? What life process can these cells carry out that a cell from another kind of multicellular organism cannot?

_____

_____

_____

_____

_____

_____

19. Most animals can survive without food for a longer time than they can survive without water. Why is water so important to animals? Why can an animal survive without food for longer?

_____

_____

_____

_____

_____

_____

_____

_____

20. One of the characteristics of living things is that they respond to external changes in their environment so that their internal environment stays as stable as possible. Why must an organism do this? Name an environmental change that an animal must respond to in order to keep a stable internal environment. What might happen to an organism if it could not adapt to an external change?

_____

_____

_____

_____

_____

Connect ESSENTIAL QUESTIONS

Lessons 2, 3, 4, 5, and 6

Answer the following question in the space provided.

21. The following picture shows the process of photosynthesis.

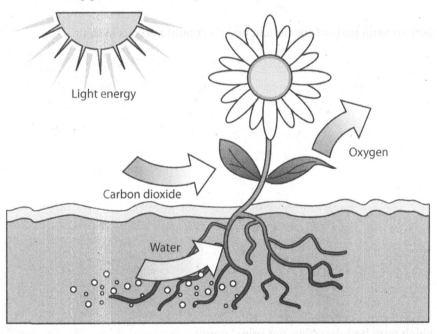

In which plant organ and organelle does photosynthesis take place? One of the products of photosynthesis is missing from the diagram. What is this missing product? Describe the role of this substance in cells. How do animals get this substance?

_____

_____

_____

_____

Cells

Key Concepts
Choose the letter of the best answer.

1. Plants make their own food during photosynthesis. In what group do plants belong?

    A. producers

    B. consumers

    C. chloroplasts

    D. decomposers

2. Which molecules make up proteins?

    A. amino acids

    B. nucleic acids

    C. phospholipids

    D. carbohydrates

3. The diagram below shows the two main parts of the human body's central nervous system.

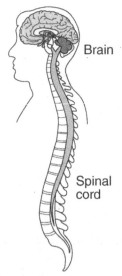

According to the diagram, which term best describes the spinal cord?

    A. cell

    B. organ

    C. tissue

    D. organ system

4. The following picture shows a prokaryotic organism.

Prokaryotic cell

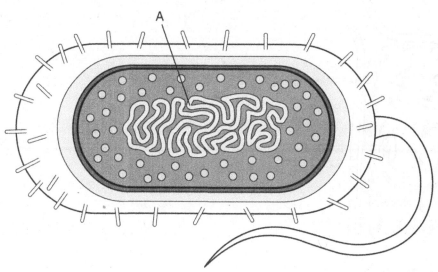

What part of the organism is labeled *A*?

A. DNA

B. cytoplasm

C. cell membrane

D. membrane-bound organelle

5. Which term describes the adaptation of cells, organs, or organ systems for a specific function?

A. structure

B. specialization

C. multicellular organism

D. level of cellular organization

6. What does a cell use to break down glucose during cellular respiration?

A. ATP

B. water

C. oxygen

D. nitrogen

7. This diagram shows a living cell.

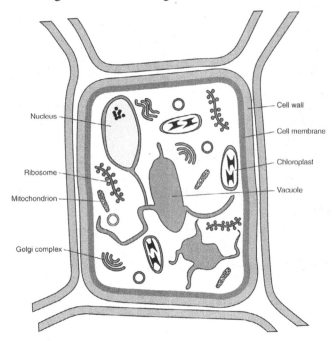

What evidence exists in the diagram to explain that it is a plant cell and not an animal cell?

A. the nucleus

B. the cell wall

C. the ribosomes

D. the mitochondrion

8. What is a difference between eukaryotic cells and prokaryotic cells?

A. Only prokaryotic cells have cytoplasm.

B. Only eukaryotic cells have a cell membrane.

C. Only prokaryotic cells have genetic material.

D. Only eukaryotic cells have membrane-bound organelles.

9. Eukaryotic cells and prokaryotic cells have some parts that are different. Which of the following would you find **only** in a eukaryotic cell?

A. a nucleus

B. a cell membrane

C. DNA in the cytoplasm

D. organelles without membranes

10. Study the diagram below to answer the following question.

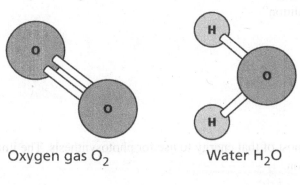

Oxygen gas O_2 Water H_2O

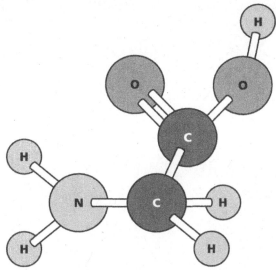

Amino acid glycine $C_2H_5NO_2$

Which of the above images is a molecule?

A. Only the first image, oxygen gas, is a molecule.

B. Only the second image, water, is a molecule.

C. Only the third image, amino acid glycine, is a molecule.

D. All three images, oxygen, water, and amino acid glycine, are molecules.

11. Some organisms consist of one cell. Other organisms consist of multiple cells. Which of the following is true of cells in a multicellular organism?

A. All cells have the same function.

B. Every cell has a different function.

C. Different types of cells have the same function.

D. Different types of cells have different functions.

12. Even when it is cold outside, the human body maintains an internal temperature of 37 °C. Which term describes the maintenance of a stable internal condition?

A. endocytosis

B. homeostasis

C. mitosis

D. photosynthesis

13. When sunlight strikes a plant, the leaves capture most of that energy to use for photosynthesis. The image below shows the process of photosynthesis in action.

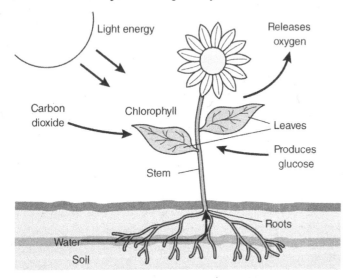

Which of these materials helps plants use energy from sunlight?

A. soil

B. roots

C. glucose

D. chlorophyll

14. What is mitosis?

A. the process by which plants make their own food

B. the process by which cells use oxygen to produce energy from food

C. the maintenance of a stable internal environment

D. the process in which a cell divides and forms two identical nuclei

15. The diagram shows parts of the human body. These parts work together to help you digest the food you eat.

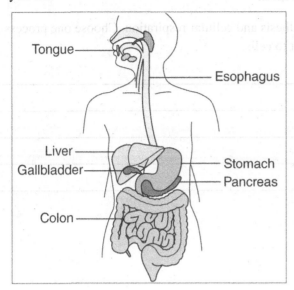

Which term best describes the entire group of parts that are labeled?

A. cell

B. organ

C. tissue

D. organ system

Critical Thinking
Answer the following questions in the space provided.

16. Explain the difference between simple and complex carbohydrates.

_____

_____

_____

_____

_____

Extended Response
Answer the following questions in the space provided.

17. Two important processes that cells use are photosynthesis and cellular respiration. Choose one process
    and describe it. Include why the process is important to cells.

    _____

    _____

    _____

    _____

    _____

Cells

Key Concepts
Choose the letter of the best answer.

1. Which of the following is an example of a producer?

    A. oak tree

    B. song bird

    C. polar bear

    D. mushroom

2. When people eat foods high in proteins, such as meat, eggs and cheese, the body breaks down the proteins into smaller molecules. What is supplied to cells when the body breaks down proteins?

    A. amino acids

    B. nucleic acids

    C. phospholipids

    D. carbohydrates

3. The diagram below shows the two main parts of the human body's central nervous system.

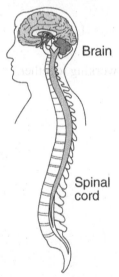

    According to the diagram, which term best describes the brain?

    A. cell

    B. organ

    C. tissue

    D. organ system

4. Alice is studying prokaryotic and eukaryotic cells.

Prokaryotic cell

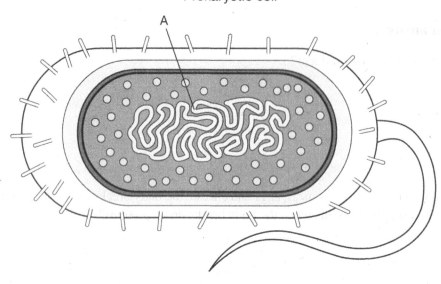

How does the part of the cell labeled *A* help Alice know that she is looking at a prokaryotic cell?

A. *A* is cytoplasm, which is found only in prokaryotic cells.

B. *A* is the cell membrane, which is found only in prokaryotic cells.

C. *A* is DNA, which is not enclosed in a nucleus, as in prokaryotic cells.

D. *A* is the nucleus, which is found only in prokaryotic cells.

5. Blood is made of different types of cells, each of which play a different role while working together. This is an example of which concept?

A. tissues

B. specialization

C. multicellular organism

D. structural organization

6. What happens to glucose inside a cell during cellular respiration?

A. The cell uses ATP to break down glucose.

B. The cell uses water to break down glucose.

C. The cell uses oxygen to break down glucose.

D. The cell uses nitrogen to break down glucose.

7. This diagram shows a living cell.

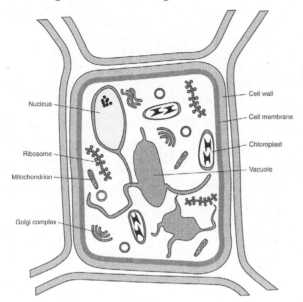

Nucleus

Ribosome

Mitochondrion

Golgi complex

Cell wall

Cell membrane

Chloroplast

Vacuole

Which statement correctly identifies the cell type and explains why?

A. This is a plant cell; the evidence is the cell wall.

B. This is a plant cell; the evidence is the nucleus.

C. This is an animal cell; the evidence is the mitochondria.

D. This is an animal cell; the evidence is the cell membrane.

8. What type of cell has membrane-bound organelles?

A. eukaryotic cells

B. prokaryotic cells

C. both prokaryotic and eukaryotic

D. neither prokaryotic and eukaryotic

9. Eukaryotic cells and prokaryotic cells have some parts that are different. Which of the following would you find **only** in a eukaryotic cell?

A. membrane-bound organelles and a nucleus

B. a nucleus and organelles without membranes

C. a cell membrane and organelles without membranes

D. membrane-bound organelles and DNA in cytoplasm

10. The following diagram shows three molecules.

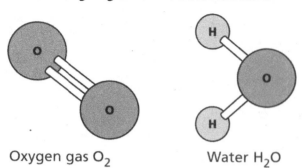

Oxygen gas O_2 Water H_2O

Amino acid glycine $C_2H_5NO_2$

Which of these statements **best** describes a molecule?

A. All molecules must contain carbon and oxygen.

B. All molecules must have two different elements.

C. All molecules are made up of two or more atoms.

D. All molecules must have at least three different atoms.

11. Jayden knows that multicellular organisms are more complex than unicellular organisms. Which of the following is a characteristic of multicellular organisms?

A. obtaining food

B. having organelles

C. being able to move

D. having specialized cells

12. The survival of a cell depends on the cell maintaining homeostasis. What is **most likely** to happen to a cell if homeostasis is not maintained?

    A. The cell will immediately divide.

    B. Cell processes will continue unchanged.

    C. The cell will eliminate wastes more efficiently.

    D. Many chemical reactions in the cell will slow down or even stop.

13. When sunlight strikes a plant, the leaves capture most of that energy to use for photosynthesis. The image below shows the process of photosynthesis in action.

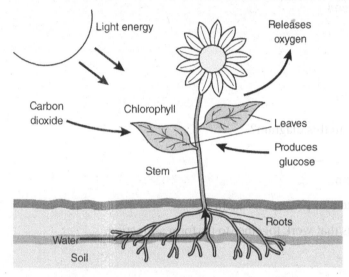

    How does chlorophyll aid in the process of photosynthesis?

    A. Chlorophyll absorbs sunlight.

    B. Chlorophyll absorbs glucose.

    C. Chlorophyll releases carbon dioxide.

    D. Chlorophyll transfers water to the roots of the plant.

14. Eukaryotic cells undergo mitosis as part of the cell cycle. What does a cell produce as a result of mitosis?

    A. two cells with identical genetic information

    B. two cells that are larger than the original cell

    C. two cells with genetic material that is different from the original cell

    D. two cells that no longer participate in the stages of the cell cycle

15. The diagram below shows parts of the human body that work together to help the body digest food.

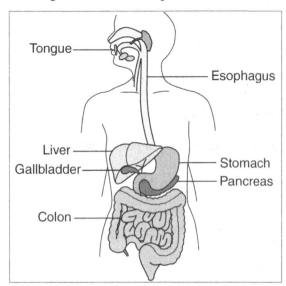

What can you conclude about the tongue from this diagram?

A. It is not part of an organ system.

B. It is made of just one type of organ system.

C. It is an organ that works as part of a system to perform a function.

D. It is made of two or more types of organs that work together to perform a function.

Critical Thinking
Answer the following questions in the space provided.

16. Explain the difference between simple and complex carbohydrates, and describe how the body uses carbohydrates.

_____

_____

_____

_____

Extended Response

Answer the following questions in the space provided.

17. Two important processes that cells use are photosynthesis and cellular respiration. Describe these two processes.

_____

_____

_____

_____

_____

Reproduction and Heredity

Choose the letter of the best answer.

1. Which of these choices best describes a pedigree?

   A. a hypothesis that explains why genes are recessive or dominant

   B. a diagram of family relationships that includes several generations

   C. an illustration that shows the genetic diversity among different species

   D. a diagram that lists alleles of two parents and shows the possible allele combinations of their offspring

2. Which of these choices describes a zygote?

   A. a structure or organ within an organism that produces gametes

   B. a cell that forms as the result of fertilization and has a full set of chromosomes

   C. a spore-like cell that is produced during asexual reproduction and can grow into a new organism

   D. a specialized cell that contains half the number of chromosomes found in other cells of an organism

3. The figure below shows a cell from an organism whose body cells each have four chromosomes.

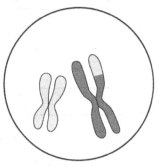

   What is shown in this figure?

   A. two chromatids

   B. four chromatids

   C. four chromosomes

   D. four chromosome pairs

4. Each pea plant has a gene that determines seed color. One version of the gene is for green seed color, and the other version of the gene is for yellow seed color. Which of these choices is another word for the two versions of the gene for seed color?

   A. trait

   B. allele

   C. genotype

   D. phenotype

5. The two mice pictured below were produced by cloning.

What do the mice have in common that makes them clones?

A. their diet

B. when they were born

C. their genetic material

D. the number of siblings they have

6. Which of these pairs identifies two steps directly involved in making a protein?

A. mutation, replication

B. replication, translation

C. transcription, replication

D. transcription, translation

7. How would living things differ if cell division took place only for reproduction?

A. All living things would be single-celled.

B. Multicellular organisms would be much smaller.

C. Living things would be more genetically diverse.

D. Multicellular organisms would be unable to repair damaged cells.

8. A timeline of discoveries related to DNA is shown below.

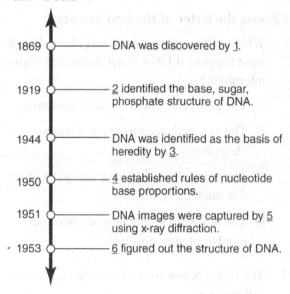

Which scientist should be placed at point 4 in this timeline?

A. Francis Crick

B. James Watson

C. Erwin Chargaff

D. Rosalind Franklin

9. Which pair shows the number of cells present both before and after meiosis II?

A. 1 and 2

B. 1 and 4

C. 2 and 4

D. 4 and 4

10. Gregor Mendel observed that two plants with purple flowers could produce some offspring with white flowers and some offspring with purple flowers. Which of the following did Mendel use to explain this result?

A. genetic mutations

B. environmental conditions

C. inherited and acquired traits

D. dominant and recessive traits

Mitosis

Choose the letter of the best answer.

1. Which of these statements most likely describes what happens if DNA is not duplicated during interphase?

   A. The new cells would be more numerous.

   B. The new cells would have too many chromosomes.

   C. The new cells would have too many or too few nuclei.

   D. The new cells would have an incorrect number of chromosomes.

2. The figure below shows the basic concepts of cell division.

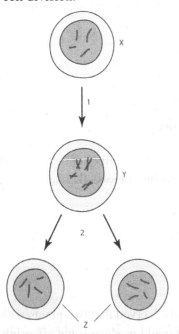

   Which of these statements describes what happens during stage 1?

   A. DNA is copied.

   B. Chromosomes unwind.

   C. The nucleus duplicates.

   D. The chromosomes separate.

3. Alla uses a microscope to look at slides of onion cells. The slides show the stages of the cell cycle. The slides are labeled and in the correct order, starting with interphase. In which slide would Alla first see chromosomes?

   A. anaphase

   B. prophase

   C. telophase

   D. cytokinesis

4. Why does cell division take place in single-celled organisms?

   A. in order for the organisms to grow

   B. to reproduce and pass on genetic information

   C. to enable the organisms to heal injured tissues

   D. to make specialized cells for different functions

5. Which of these lists presents the stages of the cell cycle in the correct order?

   A. interphase, mitosis, cytokinesis

   B. cytokinesis, mitosis, interphase

   C. mitosis, interphase, cytokinesis

   D. interphase, cytokinesis, mitosis

Meiosis

Choose the letter of the best answer.

1. If a sexually reproducing organism has 28 chromosomes in its body cells, how many chromosomes did it inherit from each parent?

   A. 7

   B. 14

   C. 16

   D. 28

2. Brandy knows that chromosomes behave differently in meiosis and mitosis. What do chromosomes do in meiosis but **not** in mitosis?

   A. Each chromosome makes a copy.

   B. The homologous chromosomes form pairs.

   C. Chromosomes line up in the middle of the cell.

   D. Chromosomes condense or shorten up before cell division begins.

3. How is meiosis related to sexual reproduction?

   A. Meiosis allows the offspring produced during sexual reproduction to grow and develop.

   B. Meiosis joins together the sex cells during sexual reproduction to produce new offspring.

   C. Meiosis produces the sex cells that join to form new offspring during sexual reproduction.

   D. Meiosis produces the body cells that join to form new offspring during sexual reproduction.

4. The diagram below shows a human cell.

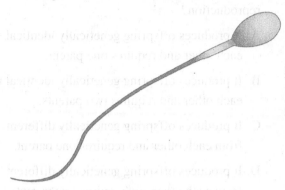

   What type of cell is this?

   A. a sex cell

   B. a body cell

   C. a cell about to go through mitosis

   D. a cell about to go through meiosis

5. How does meiosis I differ from meiosis II?

   A. The sister chromatids separate during meiosis I, but not during meiosis II.

   B. The homologous chromosomes pair up during meiosis II, but not during meiosis I.

   C. Two sex cells are produced as a result of meiosis II, but not as a result of meiosis I.

   D. Chromosome number decreases by half as a result of meiosis I, but not as a result of meiosis II.

Sexual and Asexual Reproduction

Choose the letter of the best answer.

1. Which of these statements is true of asexual reproduction?

   A. It produces offspring genetically identical to each other and requires one parent.

   B. It produces offspring genetically identical to each other and requires two parents.

   C. It produces offspring genetically different from each other and requires one parent.

   D. It produces offspring genetically different from each other and requires two parents.

2. Which of these statements correctly describes a difference between asexual and sexual reproduction?

   A. Asexual reproduction increases genetic diversity, but sexual reproduction does not.

   B. Asexual reproduction involves one parent, and sexual reproduction involves two parents.

   C. Asexual reproduction increases a species' chances of surviving unfavorable conditions, but sexual reproduction does not.

   D. The offspring produced by asexual reproduction are not identical to each other, but those of sexual reproduction are identical to each other.

3. When an organism reproduces by budding, how does the new organism start growing?

   A. from within the parent organism

   B. from the merging of two parent organisms

   C. from a spore produced by a parent organism

   D. from the outer surface of the parent organism

4. Which type of reproduction involves two parents and results in offspring that are not genetically identical to either parent?

   A. binary fission

   B. spore formation

   C. sexual reproduction

   D. vegetative reproduction

5. Look at the diagram of sexual reproduction below.

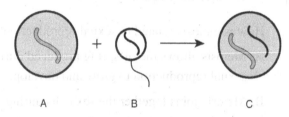

A   B   C

Which of these statements correctly describes the genetic information in the diagram?

   A. Cell A is genetically identical to cell C.

   B. Cell B contains the same genetic material as cell C.

   C. Cell C has genes from cell A and genes from cell B.

   D. Cells A and C contributed genetic material to cell B.

Heredity

Choose the letter of the best answer.

1. A scientist crosses a rabbit with short fur and a rabbit with long fur. Which of these outcomes would show that the trait for fur length is an example of incomplete dominance?

   A. All the offspring have no fur.

   B. All the offspring have long fur.

   C. All the offspring have short fur.

   D. All the offspring have medium-length fur.

2. Which of these choices is the definition of *allele*?

   A. the form of a gene that is expressed

   B. one of the alternative forms of a gene

   C. the combination of genes for a specific trait

   D. the complete genetic makeup of a living thing

3. Which of these choices describes a segment of DNA that determines a specific trait in a person, such as attached earlobes?

   A. a gene

   B. a phenotype

   C. a chromosome

   D. a characteristic

4. The diagram below shows the results of crossing a pea plant with round seeds and a pea plant with wrinkled seeds.

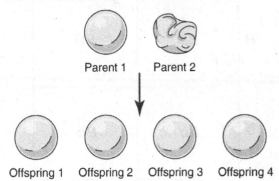

What can be determined from the results of the experiment?

   A. Smooth shape and wrinkled shape are both recessive traits.

   B. Smooth shape and wrinkled shape are both dominant traits.

   C. Smooth shape is a dominant trait, and wrinkled shape is a recessive trait.

   D. Smooth shape is a recessive trait, and wrinkled shape is a dominant trait.

5. Ryan notices that all of his friend's brothers and sisters are tall. What is the most likely explanation for this characteristic?

   A. They have tall parents.

   B. They have identical genes.

   C. They eat only healthy foods.

   D. They live in the same environment.

Name _____ Date _____

Punnett Squares and Pedigrees

Choose the letter of the best answer.

1. Examine the Punnett square below.

	B	B
B	BB	BB
b	Bb	Bb

Which of the following choices gives the alleles of the parents shown here?

A. *BB* and *BB*

B. *BB* and *Bb*

C. *Bb* and *Bb*

D. *Bb* and *bb*

2. Carrie is studying the genes of two fruit flies in her lab. She knows what alleles they have. She wants to know the potential combinations of alleles their offspring could inherit. Which of these choices would help Carrie identify the potential combinations?

A. an allele

B. a carrier

C. a pedigree

D. a Punnett square

3. Which of these statements correctly describes a difference between sex-linked disorders and other inherited genetic disorders?

A. Sex-linked disorders can be passed on from parent to child, but other inherited genetic disorders cannot be passed on.

B. Only males can be affected by sex-linked disorders, but both males and females can be affected by other inherited genetic disorders.

C. The genes for sex-linked disorders are found on a sex chromosome, but the genes for other inherited genetic disorders are found on other chromosomes.

D. The inheritance of a sex-linked disorder within a family can be traced using a pedigree, but other inherited genetic disorders cannot be traced using a pedigree.

4. Which of these choices **best** describes what a ratio shows?

A. a comparison between two quantities

B. family relationships over several generations

C. the alleles of parents and offspring for a given trait

D. the likelihood or chance that something will happen

5. Which of the following statements about pedigrees is true?

A. Boxes typically represent males and circles typically represent females.

B. Pedigrees can only be used to trace the occurrence of dominant traits.

C. Shaded shapes typically represent people who do not have a specific trait.

D. Pedigrees show all of the allele combinations that are possible in a cross.

Name _____ Date _____

DNA Structure and Function

Choose the letter of the best answer.

1. Sickle-cell anemia is an inherited disease that affects red blood cells. In people who have this disease, one amino acid is substituted for another amino acid in a blood protein. What causes sickle-cell anemia?

    A. mutation

    B. replication

    C. translation

    D. transcription

2. What is DNA?

    A. a type of molecule composed mostly of amino acids

    B. a type of molecule that performs the main functions of cells

    C. a type of molecule that speeds up the rate of a chemical reaction

    D. a type of molecule that determines the traits that an individual inherits

3. Proteins are responsible for many of our traits. How can a substitution mutation affect a person's traits?

    A. This mutation stops DNA from replicating.

    B. This mutation prevents ribosomes from synthesizing proteins.

    C. This mutation changes the number of chromosomes a person has.

    D. This mutation causes a change in the protein that forms during translation.

4. What is the purpose of replication?

    A. to make an RNA template from DNA

    B. to produce copies of a DNA molecule

    C. to move mRNA through the ribosome

    D. to change the number, type, or order of bases in DNA

5. Terrie is making a model of DNA. Which of these shapes illustrates how her model should look?

    A.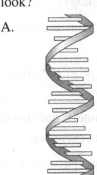

    B.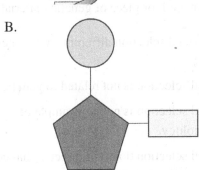

    C.

    D.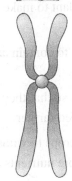

Biotechnology

Choose the letter of the best answer.

1. Artificial selection, genetic engineering, and cloning are examples of biotechnology. Which phrase **best** defines biotechnology?

   A. the application of living things and biological processes

   B. the use of computers and other electronic devices in the field of biology

   C. the development of instrumentation that can be used to study biological processes

   D. the process of creating a genetically identical organism, cell, or piece of genetic material

2. How is artificial selection different from genetic engineering?

   A. Artificial selection is not related to genetics.

   B. Artificial selection is not an example of biotechnology.

   C. Artificial selection does not directly change a single organism's DNA.

   D. Artificial selection is used to make genetically identical copies of an organisms, cell, or piece of genetic material.

3. The main goal of biotechnology is to use living organisms and biological processes to improve life on Earth. Which example would be **most** beneficial to global populations?

   A. the engineering of eggplant to make it produce fruit in winter

   B. the engineering of yeast to contain an enzyme used for making cheese

   C. the engineering of fruits so that they ripen slower and can be shipped farther

   D. the engineering of rice crops to withstand flooding and contain more nutrients

4. The dog breed shown below has been bred for many generations. It has been bred for its small size and friendly temperament.

   This is an example of which of the following types of biotechnology?

   A. by cloning

   B. selective breeding

   C. genetic engineering

   D. asexual reproduction

5. Biotechnology is the use and application of living organisms and biological processes for specific purposes. One example of biotechnology is cloning. Which of these actions can produce a clone?

   A. inserting a gene into the DNA of an existing organism

   B. removing a gene from the DNA of an existing organism

   C. developing new plants by crossing different types of plants

   D. copying the genetic material from one cell and inserting it in another cell, resulting in two genetically-identical cells

Mitosis

Climb the Ladder: *Mitosis*
Complete the activities to show what you've learned about mitosis and cell division.

1. Work on your own, with a partner, or with a small group.

2. Choose one item from each rung of the ladder. Check your choices.

3. Have your teacher approve your plan.

4. Submit or present your results.

__ **Understanding the Cycle**	__ **An Ode to Mitosis**
Make a scrapbook that shows the three stages of the cell cycle. Include at least one illustration of each stage and describe what occurs during each stage.	Write a poem about the ways that a multicellular organism appreciates mitosis.
__ **Tracking Mitosis**	__ **This Just In!**
Using the Internet, find two video simulations of mitosis. Take notes about and make sketches of the process as your watch. Then compare the strengths and weaknesses of the two simulations.	Present a news report about a new cell that has just formed. Explain how the cell formed, including the three stages of the cell cycle. Also, identify the cell as a unicellular organism or part of a multicellular organism.
__ **To Be DNA**	__ **Why, Oh Why?**
Imagine that you are the DNA in a cell that is about to go through mitosis. Present a monologue in which you describe the changes you'll go through before and during mitosis.	Create a video in which you describe the reasons that unicellular organisms go through cell division and the reasons that multicellular organism go through cell division. Include examples in your video.

Meiosis

Points of View: *Meiosis*

Your class will work together to show what you've learned about meiosis from several different viewpoints.

1. Work in groups as assigned by your teacher. Each group will be assigned to one or two viewpoints.

2. Complete your assignment and present your perspective to the class.

 Vocabulary Define *spindle, cell, chromosome,* and *duplicate* in your own words. Then find a dictionary or textbook definition. Finally, write a short paragraph using the terms that shows what you know about meiosis.

 Calculations A diploid cell from a squirrel contains 40 chromosomes. A diploid cell from corn contains 20 chromosomes. Calculate how many chromosomes are present in a haploid cell from a squirrel and corn. Then, calculate how many chromosomes are present in a diploid cell from an alligator if one of its haploid cells contains 16 chromosomes.

 Details Use a Venn diagram or other graphic organizer to show how meiosis and mitosis are alike and different.

 Illustrations Draw a sketch that illustrates the differences between the final stages of meiosis I and meiosis II.

 Analysis Explain why meiosis is important for many living things.

 Models Make a model of one of the phases in meiosis. You might use string for cell walls, macaroni noodles for chromosomes, chenille sticks/pipe cleaners for spindle fibers, and other items as needed.

Sexual and Asexual Reproduction

Tic-Tac-Toe: *Reproduction*

1. Work on your own, with a partner, or with a small group.

2. Choose three quick activities from the game. Check the boxes you plan to complete.
   They must form a straight line in any direction.

3. Have your teacher approve your plan.

4. Do each activity, and turn in your results.

__ **Plant Detective**	__ **Parent Clone**	__ **Sporific!**
Suppose you find a strange plant. How does it reproduce? Write the steps you would take to figure out whether the plant reproduces sexually or asexually.	Write a journal entry for a plant that is exactly the same as its parent. Describe the advantages of being genetically identical to your parent.	Make an illustration that shows the life cycle of a plant that produces spores. In which stage can the plant best survive harsh conditions?
__ **Diagram It!**	__ **What're the Advantages?**	__ **News Flash!**
Draw a diagram that shows how organisms reproduce by mitosis.	Make a chart showing the advantages to each kind of reproduction. Which kind allows cells to reproduce quickly and efficiently? Which promotes genetic diversity?	Imagine that a giant plant has been discovered that reproduces by budding. The buds are growing. You are a reporter. Report on what happens next.
__ **Plan a Garden**	__ **Switching Roles**	__ **Explain It!**
Design and sketch a garden. In the garden, grow some plants that reproduce sexually and some that reproduce asexually. Describe the conditions in which each type of plant will best succeed.	You notice that one of your plants usually grows new roots, but under certain conditions, it blooms. Explain why the plant may be changing types of reproduction.	Draw an explanation of fertilization for a person who is learning English. Add labels to your drawing.

Name _____ Date _____

Heredity

Climb the Ladder: *It's Hereditary*
Complete the activities below to show what you know about heredity.

1. Work on your own, with a partner, or with a small group.

2. Choose one item from each rung of the ladder. Check your choices.

3. Have your teacher approve your plan.

4. Submit or present your results.

__ **Alien Eyes**	__ **DNA's Role**
Imagine that an alien mother has purple eyes, which are recessive. The alien father has red eyes, which are dominant. What color are the offspring's eyes if aliens inherit genes in the same way as humans? _____ Explain what alleles the father might have.	Make a diagram or sketch that explains DNA's role in determining human traits. Add labels and descriptions to your diagram to make the explanation clear.
__ **Dominance Differences**	__ **Dominance Differences**
Write an entry for an encyclopedia that summarizes Mendel's findings. Include diagrams or illustrations as needed.	Make a chart that explains how complete dominance, incomplete dominance, and co-dominance are alike and different.
__ **Type Casting**	__ **Genes and Traits**
Make a poster for younger people that identifies the relationship between genotype and phenotype. Include a catchy way to remember what each term means.	Write a paragraph that explains how one gene can be responsible for many traits, and how many genes can be responsible for one trait.

Punnett Squares and Pedigrees

Climb the Pyramid: *Make a Flower*

Fill in three Punnett squares, at least one from each layer of the pyramid. After you have completed them, circle one trait in each Punnett square. List these traits at the bottom of the page. Then draw a flower that has all these traits.

1. Work on your own, with a partner, or with a small group.

2. Choose one or more items from each layer of the pyramid. Check your choices.

3. Have your teacher approve your plan.

4. Submit or present your results.

___ **R = red flower**
r = pink flower

	R	r
r	_____	_____
r	_____	_____

___ **L = long stem**
l = short stem

	L	L
l	_____	_____
l	_____	_____

___ **T = thick stem**
t = thin stem

	T	t
T	_____	_____
t	_____	_____

___ **O = oval leaf**
o = round leaf

	O	O
O	_____	_____
o	_____	_____

___ **G = solid green leaf**
g = spotted green leaf

	G	g
G	_____	_____
g	_____	_____

___ **B = big leaf**
b = small leaf

	B	B
B	_____	_____
b	_____	_____

DNA Structure and Function

Points of View: *Exploring the Double Helix*
**Your class will work together to show what you've learned
about DNA from several different viewpoints.**

1. Work in groups as assigned by your teacher. Each group will be assigned to one or two viewpoints.

2. Complete your assignment, and present your perspective to the class.

DNA

 Vocabulary Define *DNA* in your own words, and also write down a dictionary or textbook definition. Then write three sentences that use the word *DNA*.

 Details Describe the components of DNA. Make sure to use the word *nucleotide*.

 Illustrations Draw a picture of a DNA molecule and show how it replicates.

 Examples Give examples of what can happen when a mutation in a piece of DNA occurs. Explain how mutations can happen.

 Analysis Tell how the components of DNA work together.

Biotechnology

Climb the Pyramid: *The World of Biotechnology*
Climb the pyramid to show what you have learned about biotechnology.

1. Work on your own, with a partner, or with a small group.

2. Choose one item from each layer of the pyramid. Check your choices.

3. Have your teacher approve your plan.

4. Submit or present your results.

__ **Assess the Impact**

Choose one application of biotechnology you learned about. Create a list of pros and cons about it. You might consider the ethical, legal, social, financial, or environmental issues surrounding this technology.

__ **Comic Strip**

Draw a comic strip to show how humans have changed the animal or plant over time. Show the differences between the modern organism and its ancestors.

__ **Just the Facts**

Make a short presentation about how biotechnology is used in forensics or how transgenic organisms are used in scientific research.

__ **Forensics**

Research the technology behind DNA fingerprinting or other ways forensic scientists use biotechnology to help solve crimes.

__ **Transgenic Organisms**

Research a transgenic organism. Find out how the organism's genes were modified and for what purpose.

__ **Breeding the Best**

Find out about organism that has been bred by humans. It could be a pet, such as a dog, a farm animal, such as a chicken, or a crop, such as corn. How does it differ from its wild ancestors? What qualities have humans promoted through selective breeding?

Modeling Genetic Inheritance

Purpose In this activity, students will use plastic toy eggs to model the process of genetic inheritance.

Time Period 45–60 minutes

Preparation This activity will involve the use of colored plastic eggs and marbles. For each group, you will need four plastic eggs, two in one color and two in another. To avoid confusion when assigning letters for the phenotype and genotype of each egg, choose two egg colors that begin with different letters, such as red and blue eggs. Place two red marbles in one of the red eggs and two blue marbles in one of the blue eggs. For the final two eggs, combine the remaining red and blue eggs to make two mixed-color eggs. Place a red marble and a blue marble inside each. If you cannot find marbles and plastic eggs in the same colors, use dried lima beans instead of marbles. Use markers to color the dried beans to match the plastic eggs.

Safety Tips Remind students to clean up any spilled materials.

Teaching Strategies This activity can be performed individually or in small groups. Each student activity station should have four eggs: one red, one blue, and two mixed-colored. Students should work on a large flat surface so that the marbles do not roll away. Students may wish to use scratch paper to draw additional Punnett squares before recording their final answers in the data sheets.

Scoring Rubric

Possible points	Performance indicators
0–10	Appropriate use of materials and equipment
0–60	Quality and clarity of observations
0–30	Explanation and analysis of conclusions

Modeling Genetic Inheritance

Objective

In this activity you will use plastic toy eggs and marbles to model the process of genetic inheritance.

Know the Score!

As you work through this activity, keep in mind that you will be earning a grade for the following:

- how well you work with materials and equipment (10%)

- how clearly and accurately you make your observations (60%)

- how well you use your knowledge of the genetic inheritance to explain and analyze your findings (30%)

Materials and Equipment

- marbles, red and blue, divided among the eggs

- plastic eggs (4), one red, one blue, and two mixed-colored

Procedure

1. In this activity you will be answering the following question: Can genetic inheritance be predicted? Keep this question in mind as you work through the activity.

2. You are going to work with plastic eggs that contain like and unlike marbles. What combination do you think is most likely to result in the most colorful offspring?

   _____

3. Open the red and blue eggs. Notice that there are two marbles of the same color in each egg. Assign the first letter of each color as the genotype for that egg (e.g., B = blue). In this activity the eggs represent the phenotype and the marbles represent the genotype.

4. Suppose the two eggs "reproduced". Fill in the Punnett square to show how the genotypes would combine.

5. Assume that the blue color is dominant. What are the phenotypes and their probabilities? You may use scratch paper if necessary.

   _____

   _____

6. Open the two-colored egg.

7. Suppose this egg were to reproduce with one of the solid-colored eggs. Fill in the Punnett square to show the genotypes that would be created.

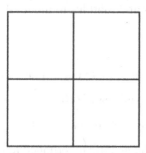

8. Remember that blue is dominant. What are the phenotypes and their probabilities in this case? You may use scratch paper if necessary.

_____

_____

9. Open the other two-colored egg. Suppose this egg were to reproduce with the other two-colored egg. Fill in the Punnett square with the genotypes that would be created.

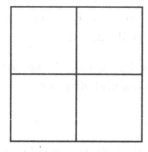

10. What are the phenotypes and their probabilities in this case? You may use scratch paper if necessary.

_____

_____

Analysis

11. Return to the hypothesis you formed in Step 2. Was your hypothesis supported? Explain why or why not.

_____

_____

_____

12. Can you exactly predict the traits that a single offspring will show? Explain why or why not.

_____

_____

_____

Unit 2: Reproduction and Heredity

Vocabulary
Fill in each blank with the term that best completes the following sentences.

1. The genetic material of all cells is _____.

2. A _____ compares or shows the relationship between two quantities.

3. A _____ is an organism, cell, or piece of genetic material that is genetically identical to one from which it was derived.

4. _____ is the process of cell division that results in the formation of cells with half the usual number of chromosomes.

5. The type of reproduction that results in offspring that are genetically identical to the single parent is known as _____ reproduction.

Key Concepts
Read each question below, and circle the best answer.

6. A mouse breeder mates a black-furred mouse with a white-furred mouse. All the offspring have gray fur. How is the trait of fur color inherited in mice?

   A. sex-linked inheritance

   B. co-dominance inheritance

   C. complete dominance inheritance

   D. incomplete dominance inheritance

7. What process does a multicellular organism use to replace its damaged body cells?

   A. mitosis

   B. meiosis

   C. replication

   D. transcription

8. The following diagram shows one way a mutation can form during DNA replication.

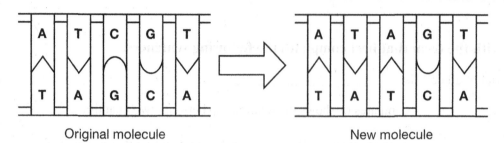

Original molecule   New molecule

What kind of mutation has occurred during the DNA replication shown in the diagram?

A. deletion   C. substitution

B. insertion   D. transcription

9. How does a sex cell differ from a body cell?

A. A sex cell does not contain chromosomes.

B. A sex cell contains homologous chromosomes.

C. A sex cell has the same number of chromosomes as a body cell.

D. A sex cell has half the amount of genetic material as a body cell.

10. How do the chromosomes at the end of meiosis I compare with the chromosomes at the end of meiosis II?

A. Chromosomes have one chromatid at the end of both meiosis I and meiosis II.

B. Chromosomes have two chromatids at the end of both meiosis I and meiosis II.

C. Chromosomes have one chromatid at the end of meiosis I and two chromatids at the end of meiosis II.

D. Chromosomes have two chromatids at the end of meiosis I and one chromatid at the end of meiosis II.

11. The following table shows the percentage of each base in a sample of DNA.

Base	Percentage of Total Bases
A	12%
C	38%
T	12%
G	38%

Which of the following statements explains the data in the table?

A. A pairs only with C, and T pairs only with G.

B. A pairs only with T, and C pairs only with G.

C DNA is made up of nucleotides that consist of a sugar, a phosphate, and a base.

D The bases in DNA are arranged in the interior of a double helix, like rungs of a ladder.

12. Which of the following is an advantage of asexual reproduction?

    A. It is a slow process.

    B. Two parents are needed.

    C. The organism can increase in number quickly.

    D. It introduces genetic diversity in the offspring.

13. The diagram below shows a cross that is similar to one of Mendel's pea plant crosses.

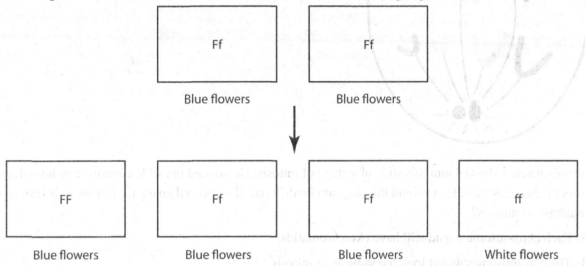

How is blue flower color inherited in the cross shown?

    A. as a co-dominant trait   C. as a dominant trait

    B. as a recessive trait   D. as an incompletely dominant trait

14. Which of the following statements correctly describes the function of cell division in unicellular organisms?

    A. Cell division allows the organism to grow.

    B. Cell division allows the organism to reproduce.

    C. Cell division allows the organism to produce sex cells.

    D. Cell division allows the organism to repair damage to the cell.

15. Which statement about zygotes, which form by fertilization, is correct?

    A. Zygotes have a full set of chromosomes, receiving half from each parent.

    B. Zygote have half the set of chromosomes from one parent only.

    C. Zygotes have two full sets of chromosomes, one set from each parent.

    D. Zygotes have half the set of chromosomes, one-fourth from each parent.

16. The diagram shows a cell during the anaphase stage of mitosis.

Justin's teacher showed him this slide of a stage of mitosis. He noticed the slide contains two homologous pairs of chromosomes. How would this diagram be different if it showed anaphase I of meiosis instead of anaphase of mitosis?

A. Each chromosome would still have two chromatids.

B. The chromosomes would look the same as in mitosis.

C. You would be able to see DNA in the chromosomes during meiosis.

D. Homologous chromosomes would be moving to the same end of the cell.

17. If the sequence of bases in one strand of DNA is ATTCGAC, what will be the base sequence on the strand that is formed during replication?

A. ATTCGAC   C. UAAGCUG

B. TAAGCTG   D. AUUCGAC

Critical Thinking
Answer the following questions in the space provided.

18. Describe the major steps of gene transcription and translation. What molecules and organelles are involved in the processes?

_____

_____

_____

_____

_____

19. Jake made a pedigree to trace the traits of straight and curly hair in his family.

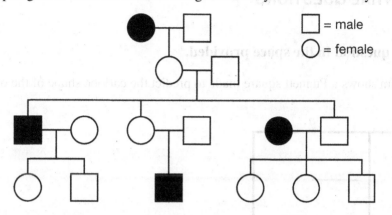

☐ = male
○ = female

A shaded circle or square in Jake's pedigree represents a person with straight hair. Is straight hair controlled by a dominant allele or a recessive allele? What led to your conclusion? How do you know that straight hair is not sex-linked?

_____

_____

_____

_____

_____

_____

20. Rachel's class is debating the impact of biotechnology on people, society, and the environment. Give one example of how biotechnology can have a positive impact. Give one example of how biotechnology can have a negative impact.

_____

_____

_____

_____

_____

Connect ESSENTIAL QUESTIONS

Lessons 4 and 5

Answer the following question in the space provided.

21. The following diagram shows a Punnett square made to predict the earlobe shape of the offspring of two parents.

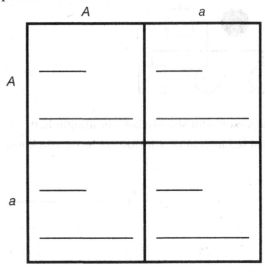

A stands for the trait of free-hanging earlobes and *a* stands for the trait of attached earlobes. Write the genotype of each offspring on the first line in each box of the Punnett square. What will be the phenotype of each offspring? Write either *attached* or *free-hanging* on the second line in each box. Describe how the trait of free-hanging earlobes is inherited. What is the expected ratio of free-hanging earlobes to attached earlobes in the offspring?

_____

_____

_____

_____

_____

_____

Reproduction and Heredity

Key Concepts
Choose the letter of the best answer.

1. The figure below shows one of the stages of the cell cycle.

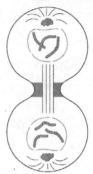

   Which answer correctly identifies the stage shown in the diagram above?

   A. mitosis

   B. anaphase

   C. interphase

   D. cytokinesis

2. Which of these statements is true of sexual and asexual reproduction?

   A. Both types of reproduction require two parents.

   B. Both types of reproduction result in offspring that are identical to one parent.

   C. Both types of reproduction enable genetic information to be passed from parent to offspring.

   D. All organisms can reproduce sexually or asexually, depending on environmental conditions.

3. Scientists must carefully weigh the risks and benefits of biotechnology. Which of these is a risk that scientists must consider when genetically engineering a plant?

   A. what kinds of nutrients the plant will need

   B. whether the plant will cause allergic reaction in humans

   C. whether the plant will grow well in different types of soil

   D. whether the plant can be crossbred with other types of plants

4. Look at the reproducing fungi shown in the picture below.

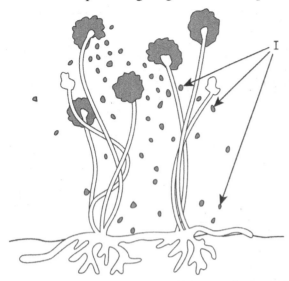

Which term describes the structures labeled I?

A. spores

B. yeasts

C. plantlets

D. parent fungi

5. How does a multicellular organism grow larger?

A. Multicellular organisms do not grow larger.

B. Individual cells in the organism grow larger.

C. The organism gains new cells from other organisms.

D. Cells in the organism divide, increasing the total number of cells.

6. What is translation?

A. the process by which DNA is copied

B. the process of transferring information from DNA to mRNA

C. the process by which mRNA directs the formation of proteins

D. the process by which one amino acid is attached to another amino acid

7. The diagram below shows a sequence of DNA.

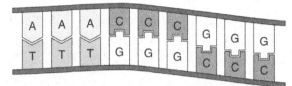

Which of the following diagrams shows the original DNA sequence with an insertion mutation?

A.

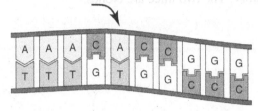

B.

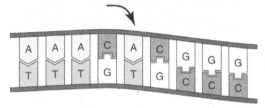

C.

D.

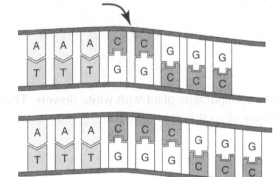

8. Alisha and Rob would like to have children. A genetic counselor tells them that they are both carriers of a certain genetic disease. What does this mean?

A. They are both immune to the disease, and it is very likely that their children will also be immune to it.

B. There is a very high probability that one or both of them will develop the disease at some point in the future.

C. They both have the disease, but there is a very low probability that they will pass it on to their children.

D. They both have an allele for the disease and could pass this allele on to their children, even though neither of them has the disease.

9. Which of the following is directly responsible for an acquired trait?

    A. genotype

    B. phenotype

    C. environment

    D. chromosomes

10. The two mice pictured below were bred in a laboratory. The two mice are clones.

    Which of these choices **best** describes clones?

    A. selectively bred organisms

    B. biologically similar organisms

    C. artificially selected individuals

    D. genetically identical individuals

11. A snapdragon plant with red flowers is crossed with a snapdragon plant with white flowers. The offspring produced have pink flowers. Which of these conditions does this cross illustrate?

    A. codominance

    B. nondominance

    C. complete dominance

    D. incomplete dominance

12. Look at the diagram below.

	A	**a**
A	**?**	**Aa**
a	**Aa**	**aa**

Which of these choices should be placed in the box with the question mark?

A. *AA*

B. *Aa*

C. *aa*

D. *AA* or *aa*, but not possible to determine which one

13. Which of these phases of mitosis takes place first?

    A. anaphase

    B. telophase

    C. prophase

    D. metaphase

14. Which of these statements best describes what happens during vegetative reproduction?

    A. A single-celled organism divides into two new organisms.

    B. A parent plant produces spores, which grow into new plants.

    C. A new plant develops from a stem or root of its parent plant.

    D. Pollen from one plant fertilizes another plant and produces offspring.

15. The diagram below shows a body cell with 4 homologous pairs of chromosomes.

During sexual reproduction, how many chromosomes will this organism transmit to its offspring?

A. 8, all of the chromosomes shown

B. 2, one pair of homologous chromosomes

C. 4, two pairs of homologous chromosomes

D. 4, one chromosome from each homologous pair

Critical Thinking

Answer the following questions in the space provided.

16. Describe the process of cell division that is associated with sexual reproduction.

_____

_____

_____

_____

Extended Response

Answer the following questions in the space provided.

17. A pair of fruit flies reproduces and has 1,000 offspring. All 1,000 of the offspring have the alleles *Gg*. What is the most likely combination of alleles for each parent? Explain your answer.

_____

_____

_____

_____

_____

_____

Reproduction and Heredity

Key Concepts
Choose the letter of the best answer.

1. The figure below shows one of the stages of the cell cycle.

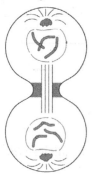

Which two stages of the cell cycle happened before the stage shown in this diagram?

A. cytokinesis and anaphase

B. interphase and mitosis

C. cytokinesis and mitosis

D. interphase and cytokinesis

2. Which of these statements is true for organisms that reproduce asexually?

A. Compared to organisms that reproduce sexually, organisms that reproduce asexually are more likely to expend energy to find a mate.

B. Compared to organisms that reproduce sexually, organisms that reproduce asexually are less likely to expend energy caring for their offspring.

C. Compared to organisms that reproduce sexually, organisms that reproduce asexually are less likely to require only one parent for reproduction to take place.

D. Compared to organisms that reproduce sexually, organisms that reproduce asexually are more likely to have offspring genetically different from themselves.

3. Scientists have produced a genetically engineered orange tree that is resistant to disease. Which of the following is the **best** example of a potential benefit to society that could result from this biotechnology?

A. increase in orange crop yield

B. reduction in orange crop yield

C. increase in the cost of orange crop

D. a change in the distribution of insects that pollinate orange flowers

4. The image below depicts fungi.

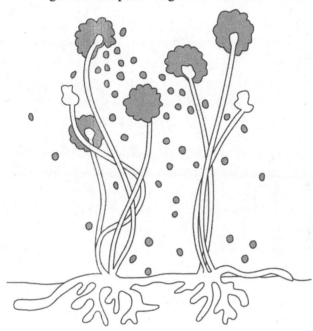

Which type of asexual reproduction is shown in the diagram?

A. budding

B. binary fission

C. spore formation

D. vegetative reproduction

5. In what way is cell division important to keeping organisms healthy?

A. Cell division makes specialized cells.

B. Cell division causes cells to grow larger.

C. Cell division replaces damaged cells with new cells.

D. Cell division is not part of keeping organisms healthy.

6. How might a deletion mutation in a gene affect the translation of that gene?

A. The mutation would not allow DNA to exit the cytoplasm.

B. The mutation would prevent amino acids from being brought to the ribosome during translation.

C. The amino acids would not be the right shape. They would not be able to assemble to form proteins.

D. The mutation would cause a different sequence of amino acids to be brought to the ribosome during translation.

7. The diagram below shows an original sequence of DNA and then a mutated sequence of DNA.

Original sequence

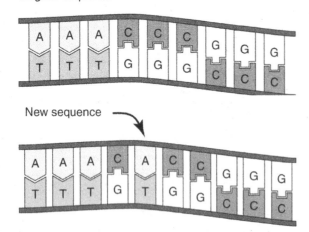

New sequence

Which type of mutation took place?

A. deletion

B. insertion

C. translation

D. substitution

8. Which of the following is true of a man who is color blind?

A. He inherited two alleles for color blindness from his father.

B. He inherited one allele for color blindness from his mother.

C. He will pass on the allele for color blindness to all of his children.

D. He has one allele for color blindness and another allele for normal vision.

9. Which of the following is an acquired trait in humans?

   A. eye color

   B. hair color

   C. blood type

   D. table manners

10. The two mice pictured below are genetically identical.

   Which term best describes the process by which these mice were produced?

   A. cloning

   B. isolation

   C. selection

   D. mutation

11. A scientist is studying the flowers of a certain plant. In one experiment, she crosses a plant that has blue flowers with a plant that has white flowers. The resulting offspring have only blue flowers. This outcome is an example of which of the following?

   A. codominance

   B. asexual reproduction

   C. complete dominance

   D. incomplete dominance

12. Look at the diagram shown below. The alleles for the parents are missing.

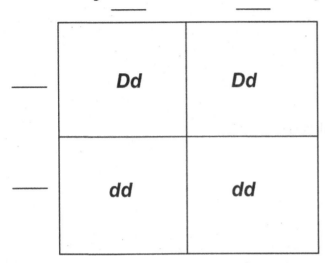

The parents in the diagram above have which of these alleles?

A. *DD* and *Dd*

B. *Dd* and *Dd*

C. *Dd* and *dd*

D. *DD* and *dd*

13. Terrell uses a microscope to look at slides of plant cells. He sees a cell with two nuclei that have visible chromosomes. In which stage of cell division is this cell?

A. anaphase

B. prophase

C. telophase

D. interphase

14. Which of these lists includes three types of asexual reproduction?

A. budding, spore formation, fertilization

B. binary fission, budding, spore formation

C. fertilization, vegetative reproduction, binary fission

D. spore formation, fertilization, vegetative reproduction

15. Brandy knows that chromosomes behave differently in meiosis and mitosis. She examines the following cell, shown below.

What feature of the cell makes it clear that the cell is undergoing meiosis?

A. Each chromosome has made a copy.

B. The homologous chromosomes have formed pairs.

C. The chromosomes are lined up along the middle of the cell.

D. The chromosomes have condensed or shortened before undergoing cell division.

Critical Thinking

Answer the following questions in the space provided.

16. Explain the relationship between meiosis and sexual reproduction.

_____

_____

_____

_____

Extended Response

Answer the following questions in the space provided.

17. A pair of fruit flies reproduces and has 1,000 offspring. All 1,000 of the offspring have the alleles *Gg*. What is the most likely combination of alleles that each parent has, and why are other combinations not likely? Explain your answer.

_____

_____

_____

_____

_____

_____

_____

Cells and Heredity

Choose the letter of the best answer.

1. Which of the following is an example of how homeostasis can cause an organism to change its behavior?

    A. A tree loses its leaves in the winter.

    B. A bear hibernates during the winter.

    C. A human shivers when exposed to cold weather.

    D. Organisms do not change their behavior because of homeostasis.

2. Which of these actions is a task shared by mRNA, rRNA, and tRNA?

    A. participating in transcription

    B. making proteins using instructions from DNA

    C. forming part of a ribosome where an amino acid chains are assembled

    D. delivering amino acids to a ribosome, where they are used to form proteins

3. A timeline of discoveries related to DNA is shown below.

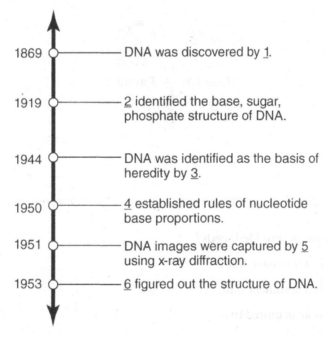

1869	DNA was discovered by 1.
1919	2 identified the base, sugar, phosphate structure of DNA.
1944	DNA was identified as the basis of heredity by 3.
1950	4 established rules of nucleotide base proportions.
1951	DNA images were captured by 5 using x-ray diffraction.
1953	6 figured out the structure of DNA.

Which scientist should be placed at point 5 in this timeline?

    A. Francis Crick

    B. James Watson

    C. Erwin Chargaff

    D. Rosalind Franklin

4. Human blood types A and B show codominance. The alleles determine what kind of antigens are produced on the red blood cells. What kind of blood cells are produced by a person that has inherited an A allele and a B allele blood?

A. type A

B. type B

C. both type A and type B

D. neither type A nor type B

5. Which term describes "one or more cells that carry out all of the processes needed to sustain life"?

A. DNA

B. organelle

C. organism

D. cytoplasm

6. A pea plant with round seeds is crossed with a pea plant with wrinkled seeds. The figure below shows the results of this cross.

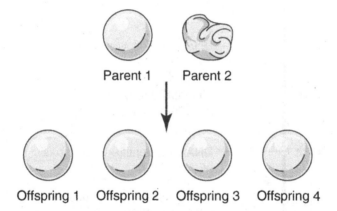

Parent 1   Parent 2

Offspring 1   Offspring 2   Offspring 3   Offspring 4

What can you conclude about wrinkled seeds?

A. The wrinkled shape is a recessive trait.

B. The wrinkled shape is a dominant trait.

C. The wrinkled shape is an acquired trait.

D. The wrinkled shape is an incomplete trait.

7. Biotechnology affects different people and groups in different ways. Which of these uses of biotechnology would be most beneficial for the environment?

A. the use of microbes to remove algae

B. a fertilizer for crops to improve growth

C. the treatment of wastewater with microbes

D. a liquid for pets to drink to eliminate bad odors

8. Which of these organisms relies on mitosis for reproduction?

   A. ant

   B. bird

   C. amoeba

   D. jellyfish

9. What form of energy is stored in food?

   A. light energy

   B. kinetic energy

   C. chemical energy

   D. mechanical energy

10. Which of the following correctly describes cellular respiration?

    A. It takes place in the chloroplasts of most plant cells.

    B. It happens only when cells need to produce more proteins.

    C. It is the process that breaks down sugars to release energy.

    D. It happens in the cellular organelles that do not have a membrane.

11. The diagram below shows a method of reproduction.

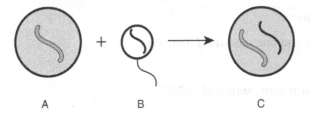

Which of these processes are represented in the diagram?

    A. asexual reproduction, budding

    B. sexual reproduction, fertilization

    C. sexual reproduction, binary fission

    D. asexual reproduction, spore formation

12. A science teacher drew a diagram of cell division.

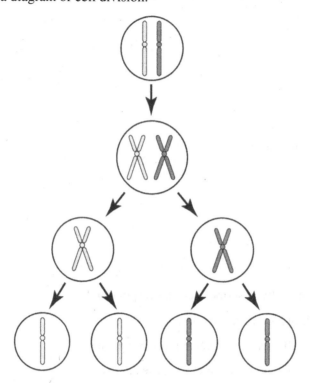

What kind of cell division is shown in this diagram?

A. one mitotic division

B. two mitotic divisions

C. two meiosis I divisions

D. one meiosis I division and one meiosis II division

13. Which of the following structures surround cells?

A. cell wall and nucleus

B. cell membrane and cell wall

C. cytoplasm and cytoskeleton

D. cell membrane and cytoplasm

14. A species of plant has a dominant gene for a tall stem and a recessive gene for a dwarf stem. How do the plant's genes and its environment influence its height?

A. Genes and environment are both major influences.

B. Genes and environment are both minor influences.

C. Environment influences the height, but genes do not.

D. Genes influence the height, but environment does not.

15. There is a relationship between breathing and cellular respiration. Breathing involves taking in oxygen and releasing carbon dioxide. How does the oxygen affect the process of cellular respiration?

    A. Oxygen and ATP combine to produce energy in the form of carbon dioxide.

    B. Oxygen and glucose combine to produce energy in the form of ATP molecules.

    C. Oxygen and hydrogen combine to produce energy in the form of ATP molecules.

    D. Oxygen and carbon dioxide combine to produce energy in the form of ATP molecules.

16. Which reason best explains why reproduction is necessary?

    A. Environmental conditions might change.

    B. Reproduction requires complex body structures.

    C. Reproduction increases the genetic variability of the species.

    D. The survival of every species depends on the ability of organisms to reproduce.

17. Which of these choices is a product of mitosis?

    A. egg

    B. sperm

    C. sex cell

    D. skin cell

18. The following diagram shows the chemical structures of oxygen gas and water.

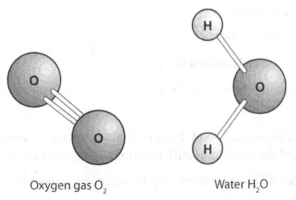

Oxygen gas O$_2$ Water H$_2$O

    Which of the above substances is both a molecule and a compound?

    A. water is both a molecule and a compound

    B. oxygen is both a molecule and a compound

    C. both oxygen and water are compounds

    D. neither oxygen nor water are compounds

19. The following picture shows a unicellular organism.

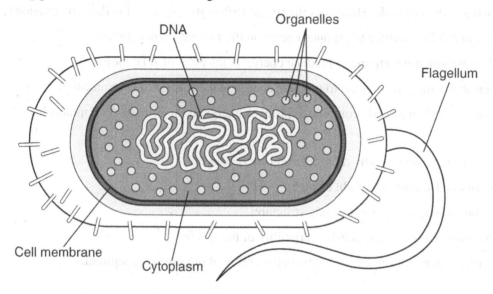

What type of a cell is shown?

A. organelle

B. membrane

C. eukaryotic

D. prokaryotic

20. Which of the following best describes a sex-linked gene?

A. a gene that is only found in males

B. a gene that is only found in females

C. a gene that is located on a sex chromosome

D. a gene that causes a sexually transmitted disease

21. Plant cells use photosynthesis to make food. Plant cells also use cellular respiration to get energy from the food they make. How is cellular respiration **different** from photosynthesis?

A. Photosynthesis produces ATP, and cellular respiration produces sugars.

B. Photosynthesis requires oxygen, and cellular respiration requires carbon dioxide.

C. Photosynthesis produces oxygen, and cellular respiration produces carbon dioxide.

D. Photosynthesis requires energy from food, and cellular respiration requires energy from the sun.

22. Eugene drew the following diagram to describe the levels of structural organization of an animal's body. He will list the cell as both the least specialized and the most numerous at the bottom of the pyramid.

Levels of Organization of an Animal's Body

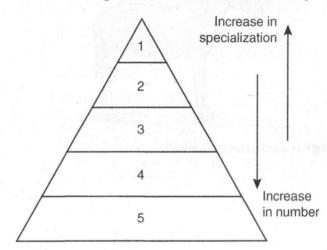

Which of the following should he list in level 1 on the diagram?

A. organ

B. tissue

C. organism

D. organ system

23. Jorge looks through a microscope and concludes that the cells he observes are eukaryotic cells. Which of the following structures did Jorge **most likely** observe before making his conclusion?

A. nucleus

B. cytoplasm

C. cell membrane

D. genetic material

24. Amanda is making a poster to describe the two types of cell division. She draws an outline of a human body on the poster. Amanda wants to show diagrams of mitosis and meiosis zooming out from the different parts of the body where they take place. Which of these choices correctly shows a location for a type of cell division?

A. bone—meiosis

B. testes—mitosis

C. ovaries—meiosis

D. stomach—meiosis

25. The animal below is a mule, which is the offspring of a male donkey and a female horse.

What kind of biotechnology is used to create mules?

A. cloning

B. selective breeding

C. genetic engineering

D. cell and tissue cultures

26. Interphase is the longest stage of what process?

A. mitosis

B. cell cycle

C. cytokinesis

D. reproduction

27. Look at the diagram shown below.

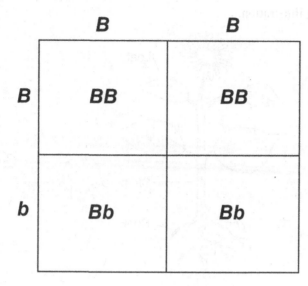

Which of these choices gives the correct ratio for the offspring predicted by the diagram?

A. 2 *BB* : 1 *Bb*

B. 1 *BB* : 1 *BB*

C. 1 *BB* : 1 *Bb*

D. 1 *BB* : 2 *Bb*

28. What will happen if the concentration of water inside a cell is higher than the concentration of water outside a cell?

A. The cell will burst.

B. Water will move into the cell.

C. The cell will remain unchanged.

D. Water will move out of the cell.

29. Jana is studying the structure and function of different parts of a flowering plant. She drew and labeled the plant shown in the following illustration.

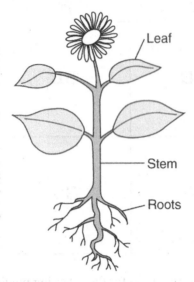

Leaf

Stem

Roots

Which statement is a function of the roots?

A. They are about 15 cm long.

B. They are connected to the stem.

C. They have tiny root hairs on them.

D. They take in nutrients from the soil.

30. Where does the exchange of materials in and out of a cell take place?

A. in the nucleus

B. in the chloroplast

C. in the chromosome

D. at the cell membrane

Name _____ Date _____

PLEASE NOTE
• Use only a no. 2 pencil
• Example: Ⓐ ● Ⓒ Ⓓ
• Erase changes COMPLETELY.

End-of-Module Test

Mark one answer for each question.

1 Ⓐ Ⓑ Ⓒ Ⓓ   11 Ⓐ Ⓑ Ⓒ Ⓓ   21 Ⓐ Ⓑ Ⓒ Ⓓ

2 Ⓐ Ⓑ Ⓒ Ⓓ   12 Ⓐ Ⓑ Ⓒ Ⓓ   22 Ⓐ Ⓑ Ⓒ Ⓓ

3 Ⓐ Ⓑ Ⓒ Ⓓ   13 Ⓐ Ⓑ Ⓒ Ⓓ   23 Ⓐ Ⓑ Ⓒ Ⓓ

4 Ⓐ Ⓑ Ⓒ Ⓓ   14 Ⓐ Ⓑ Ⓒ Ⓓ   24 Ⓐ Ⓑ Ⓒ Ⓓ

5 Ⓐ Ⓑ Ⓒ Ⓓ   15 Ⓐ Ⓑ Ⓒ Ⓓ   25 Ⓐ Ⓑ Ⓒ Ⓓ

6 Ⓐ Ⓑ Ⓒ Ⓓ   16 Ⓐ Ⓑ Ⓒ Ⓓ   26 Ⓐ Ⓑ Ⓒ Ⓓ

7 Ⓐ Ⓑ Ⓒ Ⓓ   17 Ⓐ Ⓑ Ⓒ Ⓓ   27 Ⓐ Ⓑ Ⓒ Ⓓ

8 Ⓐ Ⓑ Ⓒ Ⓓ   18 Ⓐ Ⓑ Ⓒ Ⓓ   28 Ⓐ Ⓑ Ⓒ Ⓓ

9 Ⓐ Ⓑ Ⓒ Ⓓ   19 Ⓐ Ⓑ Ⓒ Ⓓ   29 Ⓐ Ⓑ Ⓒ Ⓓ

10 Ⓐ Ⓑ Ⓒ Ⓓ   20 Ⓐ Ⓑ Ⓒ Ⓓ   30 Ⓐ Ⓑ Ⓒ Ⓓ

Test Doctor

Unit 1 Cells

Unit Pretest

1. A	5. D	9. D
2. B	6. A	10. C
3. C	7. A	
4. B	8. B	

1. A

A is correct because a leaf is an organ that traps light energy for photosynthesis.

B is incorrect because photosynthesis does not occur in the fruit.

C is incorrect because most photosynthesis does not occur in petals.

D is incorrect because photosynthesis does not occur in roots.

2. B

A is incorrect because blood is connective tissue, which is made of different types of cells.

B is correct because blood is a tissue. A tissue is a group of cells that work together to perform a specific function.

C is incorrect because blood is just one type of tissue. An organism is made of different types of tissue.

D is incorrect because blood is just one type of tissue. An organ system is made of different organs, and each organ is made of different types of tissue.

3. C

A is incorrect because the nucleus contains genetic

material and is found within a cell, not around the outside of a cell.

B is incorrect because a cytoskeleton supports a cell, allows it to move, and is found within a cell, not around the outside of a cell.

C is correct because cell membranes enclose cells and separate the cytoplasm from the environment.

D is incorrect because the genetic material is found within a cell, not around the outside of a cell.

4. B

A is incorrect because cells are made up of many molecules.

B is correct because atoms are the building blocks of molecules.

C is incorrect because molecules are made up of more than one atom.

D is incorrect because cell membranes are made up of many molecules.

5. D

A is incorrect because internal balance, not cell death, is the result of homeostasis.

B is incorrect because while cells do divide to replace dead or damaged cells, this process is not the overall result of homeostasis.

C is incorrect because cells must obtain energy to perform cell functions and maintain homeostasis.

D is correct because homeostasis results in a stable environment within the cell.

6. A

A is correct because the endoplasmic reticulum is a system of folded membranes within the cytoplasm of a cell.

B is incorrect because tiny organelles that have no membranes are ribosomes, which may be found on the endoplasmic reticulum.

C is incorrect because a rigid protective layer found outside a cell membrane is a cell wall, not endoplasmic reticulum.

D is incorrect because mitochondria, not endoplasmic reticulum, are the organelles that are surrounded by a double membrane and contain DNA.

7. A

A is correct because diffusion is the movement of molecules from areas of high concentration to areas of low concentration.

B is incorrect because exocytosis is the process by which a vesicle surrounds a large particle, moves it to the cell membrane, and releases it outside of the cell.

C is incorrect because photosynthesis is process by which plant cells convert energy from the sun into glucose and carbon dioxide.

D is incorrect because cellular respiration is the process of breaking down food to release the energy that fuels cell activities.

8. B

A is incorrect because all cells have cytoplasm.

B is correct because in eukaryotes, DNA is enclosed in a nucleus.

C is incorrect because many eukaryotes are single-celled organisms.

D is incorrect because prokaryotes, not eukaryotes, have DNA in the cytoplasm.

9. D

A is incorrect because ATP is a product of cellular respiration that both plants and animals use for energy.

B is incorrect because glucose is a product of photosynthesis, not of cellular respiration.

C is incorrect because mitochondria are the organelles in which cellular respiration takes place.

D is correct because carbon dioxide is a product of cellular respiration and is used by plants to carry out photosynthesis.

10. C

A is incorrect because proteins are made up of amino acids.

B is incorrect because calcium, not lipids, is used to repair broken bones.

C is correct because phospholipids are lipids that

contain phosphorus and make up the cell membrane.

D is incorrect because nucleic acids, not lipids, carry information in the cell. DNA is a type of nucleic acid.

Lesson 1 Quiz

1. A   4. C
2. B   5. D
3. A

1. A

A is correct because a cell has all the structures needed to perform all of the tasks necessary for life.

B is incorrect because a cell nucleus is just part of a cell and does not have all the structures needed to perform all of the tasks necessary for life.

C is incorrect because a cell membrane is just part of a cell and does not have all the structures needed to perform all of the tasks necessary for life.

D is incorrect because although a multicellular organism can perform all of the tasks necessary for life, it is composed of cells, which are a smaller unit than the organism.

2. B

A is incorrect because although both kinds of cells have cytoplasm, only eukaryotic cells have nuclei.

B is correct because a cell membrane and cytoplasm are present in both prokaryotic and eukaryotic cells.

C is incorrect because although both kinds of cells have DNA, only eukaryotic cells have membrane-bound organelles.

D is incorrect because although both prokaryotic and eukaryotic cells have a cell membrane, only eukaryotic cells have membrane-bound organelles.

3. A

A is correct because Schwann wrote the first two parts of the cell theory: organisms are made up of cells and cells are the basic unit of life.

B is incorrect because not all cells have nuclei.

C is incorrect because organs are made up of cells, but not all organisms have organs.

D is incorrect because organelles are parts within cells.

4. C

A is incorrect because it shows a prism. A prism breaks light up into the visible light spectrum and does not magnify objects.

B is incorrect because it shows a telescope. A telescope is used to look at large, distant objects, not small, nearby objects.

C is correct because it shows an early microscope. Such a microscope gave enough magnification to see the type of cells Hooke described.

D is incorrect because it shows eyeglasses. Eyeglasses would not have provided enough magnification to see the type of cells Hooke described.

5. D

A   is incorrect because not all cells have nuclei, and cells without nuclei also reproduce.

B   is incorrect because although cells can move around, movement alone does not result in cell division.

C   is incorrect because although all cells have membranes, the presence of a cell membrane alone does not result in cell division.

D   is correct because Virchow observed cell division and concluded that cells come from other cells. This is the third basic characteristic of cells, and the third part of cell theory.

Lesson 2 Quiz

1. C   4. A
2. D   5. C
3. C

1. C

A   is incorrect because proteins, not carbohydrates, are made up of amino acids.

B   is incorrect because phospholipids, not carbohydrates, form cell membranes.

C   is correct because carbohydrates provide cells with energy.

D   is incorrect because enzymes, not carbohydrates, speed up chemical reactions.

2. D

A   is incorrect because a cell is not made up of table salt.

B   is incorrect because table salt is made up of several atoms.

C   is incorrect because an element is made from only one type of atom.

D   is correct because table salt is made of different kinds of atoms (Na and Cl) chemically combined, so it is a compound.

3. C

A   is incorrect because although iron is found in the blood, it is not one of the six most common elements found in humans.

B   is incorrect because helium is not found in humans.

C   is correct because oxygen is one of the six most common elements found in humans.

D   is incorrect because although water is found in humans, it is not an element, but a molecule made up of the elements oxygen and hydrogen.

4. A

A   is correct because lipids do not mix with water.

B   is incorrect because proteins will mix with water.

C   is incorrect because nucleic acids will mix with water.

D   is incorrect because carbohydrates will mix with water.

5. C

A   is incorrect because lipids are fats, oils, and waxes that store energy.

B   is incorrect because proteins are used to build and repair body structures and to regulate body processes.

C   is correct because DNA is an example of a nucleic acid.

D   is incorrect because carbohydrates provide energy.

Lesson 3 Quiz

1. B   4. C
2. C   5. A
3. A

1. B

A   is incorrect because endoplasmic reticulum does not have a folded inner membrane or its own DNA.

B   is correct because mitochondria have a folded inner membrane, an outer membrane, and their own DNA.

C   is incorrect because nuclei do not have a folded inner membrane.

D   is incorrect because ribosomes do not have membranes or DNA.

2. C

A   is incorrect because all eukaryotic cells contain cytoplasm.

B   is incorrect because all eukaryotic cells have cell membranes.

C   is correct because eukaryotic cells can differ from each other by the quantity and types of organelles found in their cells.

D   is incorrect because eukaryotes do not contain prokaryotes—eukaryotes and prokaryotes are different types of organisms.

3. A

A   is correct because the cytoskeleton is a web of proteins that supports a cell and can help to move materials inside the cell. Some organisms use it to move the entire organism.

B   is incorrect because the nucleus is the membrane-bound organelle that contains the genetic material.

C   is incorrect because cell membranes enclose cells and separate their cytoplasm from the environment.

D   is incorrect because DNA contains the information needed for cell processes, such as making proteins.

4. C

A   is incorrect because chloroplasts perform photosynthesis; ribosomes produce proteins.

B   is incorrect because chloroplasts perform photosynthesis; vacuoles store water and food.

C   is correct because the main function of the chloroplasts is to perform photosynthesis.

D   is incorrect because the chloroplasts perform photosynthesis; the cell wall surrounds and protects plant cells.

5. A

A   is correct because ribosomes are shown in the diagram; ribosomes are the cell's smallest organelles, and they do not have membranes.

B   is incorrect because the structures are ribosomes, which produce proteins; they do not transport substances.

C   is incorrect because the structures are ribosomes, and ribosomes make proteins; mitochondria produce ATP for the cell.

D   is incorrect because the structures are ribosomes, and ribosomes do not contain DNA and do not have folded inner membranes.

Lesson 4 Quiz

1. D   4. B
2. C   5. A
3. C

1. D

A   is incorrect because the structure and function includes tissues, organs, and organ systems working together, not just different tissue types.

B   is incorrect because the jobs of tissues, organs, and organ systems are their functions, but this response does not address the structure of tissues, organs, or organ systems within an organism.

C   is incorrect because the location of tissues, organs, and organ systems define their structure, but this response does not address the function, or jobs, of tissues,

organs, and organ systems within an organism.

D   is correct because different tissues, organs, and organ systems are structured to function together to carry out life processes.

2. C

A   is incorrect because nervous tissues carry messages throughout the body.

B   is incorrect because skeletal muscles involve the bones of the body.

C   is correct because dermal tissue covers and protects structures of the body.

D   is incorrect because connective tissue holds other types of tissue together.

3. C

A   is incorrect because only animals have nerve tissue. Nerve tissue receives information about a body's environment and directs the body's response to that information.

B   is incorrect because only plants have ground tissue. Ground tissue is any plant tissue other than vascular tissue or dermal tissue.

C   is correct because both plants and animals have protective tissue. Dermal tissue covers and protects the surfaces of structures of plants. Epithelial tissue protects structures in animals.

D   is incorrect because only animals have connective tissue. Connective tissue holds organs in place and holds parts of the body together.

4. B

A   is incorrect because the stomach is an organ. It is made of many cells.

B   is correct because the diagram shows the major organs of the human digestive system. The stomach is one of these organs.

C   is incorrect because the stomach is an organ. It is made of different types of tissue.

D   is incorrect because the stomach is one of several organs that together make up the digestive system.

5. A

A   is correct because an eye is an organ. An organ is less specialized than an organism or an organ system.

B   is incorrect because an eye is an organ. An organ is more specialized than tissue.

C   is incorrect because an eye is an organ. An organ is less specialized than an organism.

D   is incorrect because an eye is an organ. An organ is less specialized than an organ system.

Lesson 5 Quiz

1. C   4. A
2. A   5. C
3. D

1. C

A   is incorrect because cells obtain energy using cellular

respiration to break down food, not from mitosis.

B   is incorrect because mitosis does not prevent bruises.

C   is correct because skin cells divide to replace dead or damaged skin cells.

D   is incorrect because skin cells divide to form new skin cells, not muscle cells.

2. A

A   is correct because all cells need energy to perform all cell functions.

B   is incorrect because all cells must be able to eliminate wastes, not absorb wastes, to survive.

C   is incorrect because some cells, such as anaerobic bacteria, do not require oxygen to survive.

D   is incorrect because most cells do not grow continuously but stop growing once they have reached a certain size.

3. D

A   is incorrect because muscle cells are required to produce shivering, and trees do not have muscle cells.

B   is incorrect because hibernation is a response of animals, not of plants.

C   is incorrect because some animals can bask in the sun to regulate internal temperatures.

D   is correct because a tree loses its leaves in winter to reduce the amount of water loss.

4. A

A   is correct because diffusion moves molecules from areas of high concentration to areas of low concentration. As a result, molecules will move into the cell.

B   is incorrect because diffusion will result in the molecules moving into the cell, where they are in lower concentration.

C   is incorrect because another cell may have a higher concentration of these molecules.

D   is incorrect because the molecules will move from the cell's external environment into the cell's cytoplasm.

5. C

A   is incorrect because the elimination of wastes is something done to maintain homeostasis, but it is not the definition of homeostasis.

B   is incorrect because the division of cells to form new cells is part of the cell cycle, not homeostasis.

C   is correct because the definition of homeostasis is the maintenance of a stable internal environment.

D   is incorrect because photosynthesis, not homeostasis, is the process by which energy from the sun is used to make food.

Lesson 6 Quiz

1. D   4. A
2. B   5. C
3. A

1. D

A is incorrect because fertilizers provide plants with additional nutrients, not energy; water is necessary for animals, but is not their energy source.

B is incorrect because glucose is produced by the plant, not in the soil; sunlight provides animals with Vitamin D, but animals get energy indirectly from the sun by eating plants or by eating other animals that eat plants.

C is incorrect because all organisms require energy whether they move or not; exercise requires energy, but is not a source of energy.

D is correct because organisms get energy from food. Plant cells produce glucose using photosynthesis, which is broken down for energy; animals get energy by eating plants or by eating other animals that eat plants.

2. B

A is incorrect because water is a starting material for photosynthesis.

B is correct because oxygen is produced during photosynthesis.

C is incorrect because chlorophyll is a pigment that enables photosynthesis.

D is incorrect because carbon dioxide is a starting material for photosynthesis.

3. A

A is correct because photosynthesis produces glucose, a sugar that stores chemical energy. Plant cells break down glucose for energy.

B is incorrect because chlorophyll is the pigment that absorbs light energy for photosynthesis.

C is incorrect because chloroplasts are the plant structures in which photosynthesis takes place.

D is incorrect because carbon dioxide is one of the starting materials plants use to produce glucose.

4. A

A is correct because glucose and oxygen are produced during photosynthesis and provide starting material for cellular respiration.

B is incorrect because heat energy and chemical energy in the form of ATP are produced during cellular respiration.

C is incorrect because carbon dioxide and water are products of cellular respiration and starting materials for photosynthesis.

D is incorrect because light energy absorbed by chlorophyll is needed for photosynthesis to occur.

5. C

A is incorrect because carbon dioxide is not stored for later use.

B is incorrect because animals do not perform photosynthesis.

C is correct because animals get rid of carbon dioxide by breathing it out.

D is incorrect because making sugar from carbon dioxide and water happens during photosynthesis, not cellular respiration. Animals do not perform photosynthesis.

Lesson 1 Alternative Assessment

Historical Cell Fiction: Writing describes a conversation that could have happened between the scientists who contributed to the cell theory. May include information about how the discoveries of Schwann, Schlieden, and Virchow contributed to the development of the cell theory.

Something in Common: Drawing includes a eukaryotic and a prokaryotic cell. The major parts of each cell are labeled. Yarn or string connects the common parts, such as the cell membrane and cytoplasm.

A Great Adventure: Guidebook relates the functions of cell organelles to rides at an amusement park. Guidebook describes each ride and what it does. It includes a color-coded map.

A Simple Cell: Poem describes a prokaryotic cell, and includes facts about a type of bacteria or archaea.

How It Works: Essay explains why it is good to be small, and includes information about a cell's surface area-to-volume ratio.

Time Capsule: Journal entries are written from the point of view of Theodor Schwann, and describe his conclusions about cells.

A Model of a Cell: Model shows each organelle in a different color and labels each organelle. The model also includes a key.

Public Service Announcement: Announcement includes information about the importance of the cell theory and includes a drawing.

A New Report: Report includes information about a single-celled organism that lives inside of the human body. Report includes the name of the organism, what it does, and where it can be found.

Lesson 2 Alternative Assessment

Vocabulary: Each vocabulary word is defined using students own words, and then each word is defined using a dictionary or textbook definition. Last, each term is used in a sentence related to cells.

Details: Descriptions explain how sugars and starches are related to carbohydrates, how amino acids are related to proteins, and how DNA and nucleotides are related to nucleic acids.

Illustrations: Drawings show an atom and a water molecule. An illustration shows how atoms and molecules are related to cells.

Analysis: Diagram explains how molecules, atoms, elements, and compounds relate to one another.

Models: Models show cell membranes and how the phospholipid molecules form this membrane.

Lesson 3 Alternative Assessment

The difference between prokaryotes and eukaryotes: The differences between prokaryotes and eukaryotes are correctly described. (Prokaryotic cells have a cell membrane, cytoplasm, and genetic material, but the genetic material in a prokaryote is not contained in a nucleus. All eukaryotic cells have cell membranes, cytoplasm, organelles, and genetic material contained in the nucleus.)

The general characteristics of the eukaryotic cell: The general characteristics of the eukaryotic cell are described. (All eukaryotic cells have cell membranes, cytoplasm, membrane-bound organelles, and genetic material contained in the nucleus. Eukaryotes also have common organelles that include mitochondria, ribosomes, endoplasmic reticulum, and the Golgi complex.)

How mitochondria function: The way mitochrondria function is correctly explained. (Mitochondria are double-membrane organelles. Many folds in the inner membrane increase the surface area inside the mitochondria available to perform cellular respiration. Cellular respiration is the process cells use to break down sugars to release energy stored in the sugar, Mitochondria transfer the energy

released from sugar to a molecule called ATP. Cells use ATP to do work.)

How the ribosomes, ER and Golgi complex work together: How ribosomes, ER, and Golgi complex work together is correctly described. (Ribosomes are organelles that make proteins. The ER is a system of folded membranes in which proteins, lipids, and other materials are made. The ER transports substances throughout the cell. Rough ER is found near the nucleus. Ribosomes on the rough ER make proteins. Rough ER delivers the proteins throughout the cell. Smooth ER does not have ribosomes and it makes lipids. Lipids and proteins are delivered to the Golgi complex from the ER to be modified and transported in a vesicle for use in or out of the cell.)

The cell wall and large central vacuoles of plants: The differences and similarities between cell walls and the large central vacuoles of plants are correctly described. (Cell walls are found outside the cell membrane and provide structure and protection to the cell. The large central vacuole in a plant cell is a membrane-bound cavity that stores water. Central vacuoles also help support the cell.)

Chloroplasts and lysosomes: The differences between chloroplasts found in plant cells and the lysosomes found in animal cells are correctly described. (Chloroplasts trap the energy of sunlight and use it to make sugar in plants. Lysosomes are responsible for digestion in animals.)

Lesson 4 Alternative Assessment

Structure and Function: Descriptions highlight two organs and how the structure of each helps it to function. Then one of these organs is analyzed to describe the type of artificial structure that would be ideal for its function and why.

Diagram: Diagram includes at least two organ systems, and describes how they work together.

Organ Journal: Journal entries describe two artificial organ systems, and include a diagram of the organs.

Human Cell Types: Descriptions explain the function of 10 human cell types. Students pick one cell type and tell why they would want to design artificial life with this cell type, or why this cell type could never be made artificially.

Building a System: Skits describe the levels of organization in a multicellular organism (cell, tissue, organ, organ system).

Instruction Booklet: Instruction booklet names the organs in an organ system and describes how the system is used.

Designer Cell: Design includes both structure and function of an imaginary specialized cell.

Life in a Pond: Poems compares adaptations of a single-celled paramecium with those of a

multicellular sunfish in a freshwater pond.

Which Tissue? Speech explains the functions of four types of tissues in humans, and makes an argument about which tissue is the most useful.

Lesson 5 Alternative Assessment

Illustrate a Poster: Poster shows the process of photosynthesis and cellular respiration. Explanations tell how these two processes are essential for cell survival and how the two processes relate.

Build a Model: 3-D model shows the processes of photosynthesis and cellular respiration. Model is labeled. Explanation describes both processes and why they are essential to cell survival.

Write a Picture Book: Picture book shows the different stages of the cell cycle. The nucleus and chromosomes are labeled. One sentence explains what happens at each stage of the cell cycle.

Be a Broadcaster: News report describes what happens as a cell divides.

Write a Skit: Skit describes passive and active transport and explains how these methods of transport help cells maintain balance.

Create an Animation: Animation demonstrates passive and active transport. Description explains both types of transport and how these help the cell maintain balance.

Lesson 6 Alternative Assessment

Evolution Quiz: Quizzes test key ideas about natural selection and answer keys provide accurate answers.

Darwin's Journal: Journal entries describe Darwin's discoveries and the ideas they inspired.

Evolution Story: Stories accurately portray the process of natural selection to show how a species evolves or goes extinct.

Scientific Dialogue: Dialogues should include the ideas of each of the four scientists, and compare their theories.

Book Cover: Covers include an appropriate image, such as a finch or tortoise, and back copy summarize Darwin's theory.

Galápagos Comic: Comics illustrate Darwin's voyage and include facts about what Darwin did and what he discovered.

Performance-Based Assessment

See Unit 1, Lesson 1

1. Diagrams should include the following cell parts: prokaryotic cell: cell wall, cell membrane, DNA, ribosome, cytoplasm (may also include flagella, pili, and other appropriate parts and labels); animal cell: cell membrane, cytoplasm, ribosomes, nucleus, mitochondria, Golgi complex, endoplasmic reticulum, lysosomes; plant cell: cell membrane, cell

wall, nucleus, ribosomes, mitochondria, Golgi complex, vacuole(s), chloroplasts, endoplasmic reticulum.

2. Accept all reasonable answers.

3. Accept all reasonable answers.

4. Sample answer: Plant cells and animal cells are most alike because both are types of eukaryotic cells. Eukaryotic cells contain a nucleus and membrane-bound organelles, and they make up multicellular eukaryotes. Prokaryotic cells are small, do not contain membrane-bound organelles, and are found as single-celled organisms.

5. Sample answer: When cells have different cell parts or numbers of cell parts, the functions that they perform will vary. For example, chloroplasts are the organelles in which photosynthesis occurs. In cells that do not contain chloroplasts, such as those in roots, the cells are not able to carry out photosynthesis.

Unit Review

Vocabulary

1. **F See Unit 1, Lesson 6**
2. **T See Unit 1, Lesson 2**
3. **F See Unit 1, Lesson 1**
4. **T See Unit 1, Lesson 3**
5. **T See Unit 1, Lesson 4**

Key Concepts

6. B	10. C	14. C
7. B	11. C	15. C
8. B	12. D	16. A
9. D	13. A	17. A

6. B See Unit 1, Lesson 1

A is incorrect because nonliving things also can contain carbon.

B is correct because only living things are made up of one or more cells.

C is incorrect because both living and nonliving things can be green.

D is incorrect because both living and nonliving objects can contain minerals.

7. B See Unit 1, Lesson 5

A is incorrect because animal cells do not need to take in DNA to maintain homeostasis; they can make DNA.

B is correct because animal cells need a constant supply of oxygen to convert food into energy.

C is incorrect because animal cells do not need chlorophyll, which is a photosynthetic pigment.

D is incorrect because carbon dioxide is a waste product of animal cells; it is not taken in. Instead, it is released.

8. B See Unit 1, Lesson 1

A is incorrect because cellular respiration *does* take place in the mitochondria.

B is the correct answer because protein synthesis, not DNA

synthesis, takes place in the ribosomes.

C is incorrect because the process of photosynthesis *does* involve the chloroplast.

D is incorrect because the Golgi complex *does* package proteins.

9. D See Unit 1, Lesson 2

A is incorrect because lipids cannot mix with water, although they are energy sources.

B is incorrect because chlorophyll is not used as an energy source by cells; it is a photosynthetic pigment.

C is incorrect because nucleic acids are not an energy source in cells.

D is correct because many carbohydrates, such as sugars, are soluble in water and are the cells' main energy source.

10. C See Unit 1, Lesson 5

A is incorrect because osmosis is the simple movement of water across a selectively permeable membrane and does not require energy.

B is incorrect because diffusion is the simple movement of materials along a concentration gradient and does not require energy.

C is correct because energy is required to move materials against a concentration gradient.

D is incorrect because passive transport occurs without the use of energy.

11. C See Unit 1, Lesson 6

A is incorrect because photosynthesis takes place in chloroplasts. The diagram shows a mitochondrion.

B is incorrect because protein synthesis takes place in ribosomes. The diagram shows a mitochondrion.

C is correct because the organelle shown is a mitochondrion, the site of cellular respiration.

D is incorrect because the Golgi complex packages and distributes proteins. The diagram shows a mitochondrion.

12. D See Unit 1, Lesson 4

A is incorrect because the digestive system breaks down food and absorbs nutrients in animals. It does not transport water and nutrients around the body.

B is incorrect because the excretory system removes wastes from an animal's body.

C is incorrect because the respiratory system takes in oxygen and removes carbon dioxide from an animal's body.

D is correct because the circulatory system transports nutrients to cells and removes wastes. This function is similar to the vascular tissue of plants. Xylem and phloem transport water and nutrients throughout a plant.

13. A See Unit 1, Lesson 1 and Lesson 5

A is correct because unicellular organisms have only one cell, so cell division is reproduction. Multicellular organisms grow larger by making more cells.

B is incorrect because cell division in multicellular organisms makes more cells, but does not make more organisms.

C is incorrect because cell division in multicellular organisms makes more cells but does not result in more multicellular organisms.

D is incorrect because unicellular organisms do not grow larger by making new cells.

14. C See Unit 1, Lesson 3

A is incorrect because mitosis, the division of a nucleus, does not occur in prokaryotes.

B is incorrect because no cell can function without proteins.

C is correct because both prokaryotic and eukaryotic cells have ribosomes and cell membranes.

D is incorrect because all organisms, including prokaryotes, contain DNA.

15. C See Unit 1, Lesson 4

A is incorrect because animals do not make food. The stomach breaks down food that the animal takes in.

B is incorrect because an organ is a collection of several

tissues, each of which is made of similar cell types.

C is correct because an organ is a collection of different tissues that each carries out a specialized function.

D is incorrect because neither a leaf nor a stomach is involved in gas exchange.

16. A See Unit 1, Lesson 1

A is correct because cell model A has the most cell membrane compared to its volume. Therefore it has the largest surface-area-to-volume ratio, allowing nutrients and water to be efficiently transported into the cell.

B is incorrect because the amount of cell membrane compared to cell volume in cell model B is not the greatest.

C is incorrect because the amount of cell membrane compared to cell volume in cell model C is not the greatest.

D is incorrect because the amount of cell membrane compared to cell volume in cell model D is the smallest of the four cell models.

17. A See Unit 1, Lesson 4

A is correct because each type of cell in a multicellular organism performs a specialized function but cannot perform all functions.

B is incorrect because a cell does not switch from one function to another in sequence.

C is incorrect because even cells that are not specialized have a complex structure.

D is incorrect because specialization means that a cell cannot do everything.

Critical Thinking

18. See Unit 1, Lesson 3

- Dimitri likely identified the cell based on his observation of a cell wall, a central vacuole, and the presence of chloroplasts.

- Dimitri is correct because *none of these organelles are found in animal cells.*

- This cell *contains chloroplasts, so can carry out photosynthesis.* Animal cells cannot photo-synthesize.

19. See Unit 1, Lesson 2

- Water is vital for life because *most of the substances important to life are dissolved in water within cells and in the body, making them easier to transport across cell membranes. As a result, many life processes require water.* Without water, life's processes will stop.

- *Extra energy from food can be stored in the body in the form of carbohydrate and fat, so an animal could continue to function for a while* without taking food in. However *animals cannot make water and they cannot store it in a similar way that they can store food energy. They must take in water from an external source.*

20. See Unit 1, Lesson 5

- *Organisms must respond to environmental changes in order to maintain a stable internal environment. This process is called homeostasis.*

- *A drop in environmental temperature is a change in the environment that an animal would have to respond to in order to maintain normal body temperature. An animal could move to a warmer spot, or a person could put on more clothes.*

- The animal may get sick because its body is no longer able to maintain homeostasis. If there is a large change in the external environment that the organism cannot adapt to, it may die.

Connect Essential Questions

21. See Unit 1, Lesson 3, Lesson 4, Lesson 5, and Lesson 6

Sample answer:

- *Photosynthesis takes place in leaves and within the chloroplasts of the leaf cells.*

- *The missing product in the photosynthesis diagram is glucose.*

- *Glucose is broken down during cellular respiration. The energy in the chemical bonds of glucose is transferred to ATP, which the cell uses to fuel its life functions.*

- *Animals cannot make their own food, so they must take it into their bodies. Non photosynthesizing organisms do this by eating plants.*

Energy from plant food in the form of carbohydrates fuels life processes in animals.

Unit Test A
Key Concepts

1. A	6. C	11. D
2. A	7. B	12. B
3. B	8. D	13. D
4. A	9. A	14. D
5. B	10. D	15. D

1. A

A is correct because organisms that can make their own food are producers.

B is incorrect because consumers eat other organisms for food.

C is incorrect because chloroplasts are the organelle in which plants perform photosynthesis.

D is incorrect because decomposers break down dead organisms or the wastes of other organisms.

2. A

A is correct because the body breaks down proteins into amino acids, which form new protein chains that are supplied to the body.

B is incorrect because nucleic acids carry information in the cell, for example, to tell the body what proteins to make.

C is incorrect because phospholipids are lipids, or fat molecules, not proteins.

D is incorrect because carbohydrates are molecules such as sugars, starches, and fibers that are a source of

energy for the body, not
proteins.

3. B

A is incorrect because the spinal
cord is an organ, and an
organ is made of many cells.

B is correct because the spinal
cord is an organ that is part of
the nervous system.

C is incorrect because the spinal
cord is an organ, and it is
made of different types of
tissue.

D is incorrect because the spinal
cord is an organ which is part
of an organ system.

4. A

A is correct because the DNA
of a prokaryotic organism is
not enclosed in a nucleus.

B is incorrect because the
cytoplasm is all the
nonnuclear material inside
the cell.

C is incorrect because the cell
membrane is the surface of
the cell.

D is incorrect because a
prokaryotic cell does not
have membrane-bound
organelles.

5. B

A is incorrect because structure
refers to a cell, organ, or
organ system's location, or
arrangement, in an organism.

B is correct because
specialization is the term that
describes the adaptation of
cells, organs, or organ
systems for a specific
function.

C is incorrect because the term
multicellular organism refers
to an organism with more
than one cell.

D is incorrect because levels of
cellular organization
describes the complexity of
an organism's cell, tissue,
and organ structure.

6. C

A is incorrect because ATP is a
product of a cell breaking
down glucose and is not a
starting material of cellular
respiration.

B is incorrect because water is a
product of a cell breaking
down glucose and is not a
starting material of cellular
respiration.

C is correct because oxygen is a
starting material that a cell
uses to break down glucose
during cellular respiration.

D is incorrect because cells do
not use nitrogen as a starting
material to break down
glucose during cellular
respiration.

7. B

A is incorrect because both
plant and animal cells have
nuclei.

B is correct because plant cells
have cell walls, and animal
cells do not.

C is incorrect because both
plant and animal cells have
ribosomes.

D is incorrect because both
plant and animal cells have
mitochondria.

8. D

A is incorrect because both
prokaryotic cells and
eukaryotic cells have
cytoplasm.

B is incorrect because both
prokaryotic and eukaryotic
cells have a cell membrane.

C is incorrect because genetic
material is present in both
types of cells.

D is correct because eukaryotic
cells have membrane-bound
organelles, and prokaryotic
cells do not.

9. A

A is correct because a nucleus
is found only in eukaryotic
cells.

B is incorrect because cell
membranes are found in both
prokaryotic and eukaryotic
cells.

C is incorrect because DNA in
the cytoplasm is a
characteristic of prokaryotic
cells.

D is incorrect because
organelles without
membranes are found only in
prokaryotic cells.

10. D

A is incorrect because all three
images show molecules.
Oxygen gas is a molecule,
but so are the other two
images.

B is incorrect because all three
images are molecules. Water
is a molecule, but so are
oxygen gas and the amino
acid glycine.

C is incorrect because all three
images show molecules.

Amino acid glycine is a molecule, but so are oxygen gas and water.

D is correct because all three images show molecules. A molecule is any group of atoms bonded together, so oxygen gas, water, and amino acid glycine are each examples of molecules.

11. D

A is incorrect because a multicellular organism contains groups of cells that have the same function.

B is incorrect because in a multicellular organism, different types of cells have different functions.

C is incorrect because a multicellular organism contains specialized cells that have different functions.

D is correct because a multicellular organism contains different types of cells, and each type has a specialized function.

12. B

A is incorrect because endocytosis is the process by which cells bring materials into the cytoplasm.

B is correct because maintaining a stable internal temperature is an example of homeostasis.

C is incorrect because mitosis is the process of cell division.

D is incorrect because photosynthesis is the process by which plants make food.

13. D

A is incorrect because the soil provides water and nutrients for plants but does not directly take part in photosynthesis.

B is incorrect because the roots take in water and nutrients from the soil but do not directly take part in photosynthesis.

C is incorrect because glucose is a product of photosynthesis, the process which uses energy from sunlight.

D is correct because the chlorophyll inside plant cells converts light energy from the sun, which is used to combine carbon dioxide and water to produce glucose and oxygen.

14. D

A is incorrect because this describes photosynthesis.

B is incorrect because this describes cellular respiration.

C is incorrect because this describes homeostasis.

D is correct because mitosis is cell division that forms two new nuclei that are identical to each other.

15. D

A is incorrect because each labeled part is an organ, and organs are made up of many cells.

B is incorrect because many organs are shown, not just one.

C is incorrect because the group contains many kinds of tissue, not just one.

D is correct because the diagram shows the major parts of the human digestive system. Each of the major parts is an organ, and together they make up an organ system.

Critical Thinking
16

• simple carbohydrates: one or a few sugar molecules linked together

• complex carbohydrates: many, even hundreds, of sugar molecules linked together

Extended Response
17.

One of the following:

• photosynthesis: process used to obtain energy from the sun; makes food for plants; important for cells because food provides energy to fuel activities in the plant

• cellular respiration: breaks down food and stores energy in ATP; releases carbon dioxide; important because produces energy to fuel activities in the plant

Unit Test B
Key Concepts

1. A	6. C	11. D
2. A	7. A	12. D
3. B	8. A	13. A
4. C	9. A	14. A
5. B	10. C	15. C

1. A

A is correct because an oak tree is a plant; plants are producers.

B is incorrect because a song bird is an animal; animals are consumers.

C is incorrect because a polar bear is an animal; animals are consumers.

D is incorrect because a mushroom is a fungus; fungi are decomposers.

2. A

A is correct because the body breaks down proteins into amino acids, which form new protein chains that are supplied to the body.

B is incorrect because nucleic acids tell the body what proteins to make.

C is incorrect because phospholipids are lipids, not proteins.

D is incorrect because carbohydrates are a source of energy for the body, not a product of the breakdown of proteins.

3. B

A is incorrect because the brain is an organ, and an organ is made of many cells.

B is correct because the brain is an organ that is part of the nervous system.

C is incorrect because the brain is an organ, and it is made of different types of tissue.

D is incorrect because the brain is an organ which is part of an organ system.

4. C

A is incorrect because both prokaryotic and eukaryotic cells have cytoplasm, and the label is pointing to DNA.

B is incorrect because both types of cells have a cell membrane, and the label is pointing to DNA.

C is correct because the label is pointing to DNA that is not enclosed in a nucleus. This is a characteristic of prokaryotic cells.

D is incorrect because prokaryotic cells do not have a nucleus, and the label is pointing to DNA in the cytoplasm.

5. B

A is incorrect because though blood is a tissue, the term itself doesn't describe cells working together.

B is correct because the different cells playing roles to allow blood to function is an example of the concept of specialization.

C is incorrect because the term multicellular organism does not describe different types of cells working together.

D is incorrect because structural organization is the term used to describe cells, tissues, organs, organ systems, and organisms in terms of complexity.

6. C

A is incorrect because ATP is a product of a cell breaking down glucose and is not a

starting material of cellular respiration.

B is incorrect because water is a product of a cell breaking down glucose and is not a starting material of cellular respiration.

C is correct because oxygen is a starting material that a cell uses to break down glucose during cellular respiration.

D is incorrect because cells do not use nitrogen as a starting material to break down glucose during cellular respiration.

7. A

A is correct because plant cells have cell walls, and animal cells do not.

B is incorrect because although the cell is a plant cell, both plant and animal cells have nuclei.

C is incorrect because the cell has structures, such as a cell wall, that are found only in plant cells.

D is incorrect because the diagram shows chloroplasts and a cell wall, which means that this is a plant cell.

8. A

A is correct because only eukaryotic, not prokaryotic, cells have membrane-bound organelles.

B is incorrect because eukaryotic cells have membrane-bound organelles.

C is incorrect because only eukaryotic cells have membrane-bound organelles.

D is incorrect because prokaryotic cells do not have membrane-bound organelles, but eukaryotic cells do.

9. A

A is correct because both membrane-bound organelles and a nucleus are found in a eukaryotic cell.

B is incorrect because organelles without membranes are found only in prokaryotic cells.

C is incorrect because although a cell membrane is found in both types of cells, organelles without membranes are found only in prokaryotic cells.

D is incorrect because DNA in cytoplasm is a characteristic of prokaryotic cells.

10. C

A is incorrect because many molecules contain elements other than carbon and oxygen.

B is incorrect because molecules can be made up of just one type of atom.

C is correct because molecules are combinations of two or more atoms.

D is incorrect because molecules can be made up of just one type of atom.

11. D

A is incorrect because both types of organisms have the ability to obtain food.

B is incorrect because both types of organisms can have organelles.

C is incorrect because both types of organisms have the ability to move.

D is correct because unicellular organisms do not have specialized cells.

12. D

A is incorrect because a cell that is not maintaining homeostasis is unlikely to divide.

B is incorrect because cell processes do not continue operating normally if homeostasis is not maintained.

C is incorrect because if a cell is not maintaining homeostasis, it will be less able to eliminate wastes efficiently.

D is correct because internal conditions must remain stable in order for cell processes to continue operating normally.

13. A

A is correct because chlorophyll aids photosynthesis by absorbing sunlight, which is then used to make food for the plant.

B is incorrect because chlorophyll absorbs sunlight, not glucose.

C is incorrect because the plant absorbs carbon dioxide. It does not releases it. Further, this is not a function performed by chlorophyll.

D is incorrect because the roots of the plant absorb water and transfer it to the rest of the plant. Chlorophyll absorbs sunlight.

14. A

A is correct because each new cell has the same genetic information as the original cell.

B is incorrect because the two new cells are smaller than the original cell. They will eventually grow to the size of the original cell.

C is incorrect because each new cell receives a complete set of genetic information that was present in the original cell.

D is incorrect because the two cells will continue the cell cycle until they die.

15. C

A is incorrect because the diagram shows that the tongue is an organ that is part of the digestive system. An organ is made of different types of cells.

B is incorrect because the tongue is an organ. An organ is part of an organ system.

C is correct because the diagram shows that the tongue is an organ that is part of the digestive system. An organ is made up of two or more types of tissue that work together to perform a specific function.

D is incorrect because the diagram shows that the tongue is an organ that is part of the digestive system.

Critical Thinking

16.

- simple carbohydrates: one or a few sugar molecules linked together

- complex carbohydrates: many, even hundreds, of sugar molecules linked together

- description of how body uses carbohydrates (e.g., *The body uses carbohydrates for energy and to store energy; etc.*)

Extended Response

17.

- simple carbohydrates: one or a few sugar molecules linked together

- complex carbohydrates: many, even hundreds, of sugar molecules linked together

- description of how body uses carbohydrates (e.g., *The body uses carbohydrates for energy and to store energy; etc.*)

Unit 2 Reproduction and Heredity

Unit Pretest

1. B	5. C	9. C
2. B	6. D	10. D
3. B	7. A	
4. C	8. C	

1. B

A is incorrect because a pedigree is a diagram of relationships that exist in a family, but it does not explain dominance.

B is correct because a pedigree shows relationships within a family and includes two or more generations.

C is incorrect because a pedigree is a diagram of relationships that exist in a family. It does not describe genetic diversity among different species.

D is incorrect because this choice describes a Punnett square.

2. B

A is incorrect because this choice describes a testis in a male or an ovary in a female.

B is correct because a zygote is the cell that forms after a sperm fertilizes an egg. It has a full set of chromosomes because it contains the chromosomes from both the sperm and egg.

C is incorrect because a zygote is produced by sexual reproduction and is not spore-like.

D is incorrect because this choice describes a sperm or egg cell.

3. B

A is incorrect because there are four chromatids. Each chromosome consists of two chromatids.

B is correct because there are two chromosomes, each consisting of a pair of sister chromatids.

C is incorrect because there are only two chromosomes. Each chromosome consists of two sister chromatids.

D is incorrect because there are four chromatids.

4. C

A is incorrect because a trait is a characteristic of an organism that can be observed or detected.

B is incorrect because *allele* is defined as one of the

alternative forms of a gene, and not both forms.

C is correct because a genotype consists of the two alleles for a particular trait.

D is incorrect because the phenotype is the expressed trait.

5. C

A is incorrect because their identical genetic material, not their diet, makes them clones.

B is incorrect because two mice that are not clones can be born on the same day.

C is correct because the mice have the same genome.

D is incorrect because two mice that are not clones can have the same number of siblings.

6. D

A is incorrect because mutation is a change in DNA, and replication is the process by which DNA makes copies of itself; neither is directly involved in making a protein.

B is incorrect because replication is not directly involved in the formation of proteins.

C is incorrect because replication is not directly involved in the formation of proteins.

D is correct because transcription is the process by which DNA makes RNA. Translation is the process by which RNA is responsible for directing the incorporation of amino acids into a protein.

7. A

A is correct because multicellular living things develop through cell division for growth and repair. If cell division for this purpose did not take place, multicellular organisms would not develop.

B is incorrect because multicellular organisms would not develop without cell division for growth and repair.

C is incorrect because then all living things would be single-celled. Cell division in single-celled organisms produces genetically identical offspring. It does not increase diversity.

D is incorrect because multicellular organisms would not develop without cell division for growth and repair.

8. C

A is incorrect because Francis Crick was one of the co-discoverers of the double-helix structure of DNA, which is point 6 in the timeline.

B is incorrect because James Watson was one of the co-discoverers of the structure of the DNA molecule, at point 6 in the timeline.

C is correct because Erwin Chargaff discovered the rules by which the nucleotide bases in DNA form pairs; his name belongs at point 4 in the timeline.

D is incorrect because Rosalind Franklin used x-ray diffraction to make images of the shape of DNA, which is point 5 in the timeline.

9. C

A is incorrect because this pair shows the numbers of cells before and after meiosis I or mitosis.

B is incorrect because this pair shows the numbers of cells before and after both meiosis I and meiosis II are complete.

C is correct because two cells divide to become four cells in meiosis II.

D is incorrect because this pair shows no increase in cell number, which indicates that no cell division has taken place.

10. D

A is incorrect because Mendel explained the results by identifying dominant and recessive traits in the plants, not mutations. His studies did not directly address mutations.

B is incorrect because Mendel's findings were based on dominant and recessive traits. He did not recognize that the environment could affect the expression of genes.

C is incorrect because acquired traits are not inherited, and flower color is an inherited trait.

D is correct because Mendel explained the differences in the traits he observed by concluding that plants have both dominant and recessive traits.

Lesson 1 Quiz

1. D   4. B
2. A   5. A
3. B

1. D

A is incorrect because the number of cells produced would be two or less.

B is incorrect because the number of chromosomes would be reduced if DNA was not duplicated.

C is incorrect because the number of nuclei would likely not be affected by the error.

D is correct because if DNA is not duplicated, the chromosome pairs would not separate correctly. The resulting nuclei would have too few chromosomes.

2. A

A is correct because before cells undergo mitosis, DNA must be copied. Early in mitosis, sister chromosomes form.

B is incorrect because chromosomes do not unravel until interphase, during which DNA is part of chromatin in the DNA-protein complex.

C is incorrect because mitosis has not happened yet, so there is still only one nucleus.

D is incorrect because chromosomes separate at mitosis, which has not happened yet.

3. B

A is incorrect because chromosomes would be visible in anaphase, but this is not the first stage of the cell cycle in which they are visible.

B is correct because during prophase, the first phase of mitosis, the chromatin condenses into chromosomes.

C is incorrect because chromosomes would be visible during cytokinesis, but this is the last stage in which they are visible.

D is incorrect because chromosomes are visible during telophase, but this is not the first stage in which they are visible.

4. B

A is incorrect because cell division for growth takes place in multicellular organisms, not single-celled organisms.

B is correct because single-celled organisms undergo cell division for reproduction, enabling them to transmit their genetic information to the next generation.

C is incorrect because a multicellular organism can undergo cell division to repair an injury, but single-celled organisms cannot.

D is incorrect because multicellular, not single-celled, organisms undergo cell division for specialization.

5. A

A is correct because interphase is followed by mitosis, which is followed by cytokinesis.

B is incorrect because cytokinesis follows mitosis.

C is incorrect because mitosis is followed by cytokinesis.

D is incorrect because interphase is followed by mitosis.

Lesson 2 Quiz

1. B   4. A
2. B   5. D
3. C

1. B

A is incorrect because an organism inherits half of its chromosomes from each parent. Half of 28 is 14, not 7.

B is correct because 14 is half of 28. This is the amount of chromosomes the organism would inherit from each parent during sexual reproduction.

C is incorrect because an organism inherits half of its chromosomes from each parent. Half of 28 is 14, not 16.

D is incorrect because an organism inherits half of its chromosomes from each parent, not the full set of chromosomes.

2. B

A is incorrect because chromosomes are duplicated during both meiosis and mitosis.

B is correct because homologous chromosomes do not pair up during mitosis.

C is incorrect because chromosomes line up along the equatorial plate during both types of cell division.

D is incorrect because condensation of chromosomes happens before both meiosis and mitosis.

3. C

A is incorrect because this choice describes the role of mitosis.

B is incorrect because this choice describes the role of fertilization.

C is correct because meiosis produces eggs and sperm.

D is incorrect because meiosis produces sex cells, not body cells. In addition, sex cells, not body cells, join to form new offspring.

4. A

A is correct because it is a sperm cell.

B is incorrect because sperm cells are sex cells, not body cells.

C is incorrect because body cells can undergo mitosis or meiosis, but sex cells are the product of meiosis.

D is incorrect because it is a sex cell that has just undergone meiosis.

5. D

A is incorrect because the sister chromatids of a chromosome separate during meiosis II.

B is incorrect because the homologous chromosomes pair up in meiosis I when the recombination of genetic material between homologous pairs takes place.

C is incorrect because two sex cells are produced as a result of meiosis I, and four sex cells are produced as a result of meiosis II.

D is correct because each of the two cells at the end of meiosis I has half the chromosome number. The two chromatids of each chromosome separate during meiosis II.

Lesson 3 Quiz

1. A   4. C
2. B   5. C
3. D

1. A

A is correct because asexual reproduction is a type of reproduction that requires only one parent and results in genetically identical offspring.

B is incorrect because asexual reproduction requires only one parent.

C is incorrect because asexual reproduction produces genetically identical offspring.

D is incorrect because asexual reproduction produces genetically identical offspring and requires only one parent.

2. B

A is incorrect because sexual reproduction increases genetic diversity, but asexual reproduction does not.

B is correct because asexual reproduction requires only one parent, and sexual reproduction requires two parents.

C is incorrect because sexual reproduction increases a species' chances of surviving unfavorable conditions, but asexual reproduction does not.

D is incorrect because the offspring produced by sexual reproduction are not identical to each other, but those of asexual reproduction are identical to each other.

3. D

A is incorrect because in budding, a new organism grows on the outside of the parent organism, not within the parent organism.

B is incorrect because the merging of two parent organisms would be an example of sexual reproduction, and budding is asexual.

C is incorrect because budding does not involve the formation of a spore.

D is correct because in budding, a new organism grows from the outer surface of the parent organism.

4. C

A is incorrect because in binary fission, one organism divides

asexually to form two genetically identical organisms.

B is incorrect because spore formation involves only one parent and produces offspring that are genetically identical to the parent.

C is correct because sexual reproduction requires two parents and produces offspring that have characteristics of both parents.

D is incorrect because vegetative reproduction is a type of asexual reproduction, so the offspring are genetically identical to the parent.

5. C

A is incorrect because after fertilization, the zygote (cell C) is not genetically identical to the egg (cell A).

B is incorrect because after fertilization, the zygote (cell C) is not genetically identical to the sperm (cell B).

C is correct because after fertilization, the zygote (cell C) has a full set of chromosomes. Half of these chromosomes are from the sperm (cell B), and the other half are from the egg (cell A).

D is incorrect because cell B is the sperm, which contributes genes to cell C (the zygote).

Lesson 4 Quiz

1. D   4. C
2. B   5. A
3. A

1. D

A   is incorrect because the offspring would have a fur length between that of the parents.

B   is incorrect because this would indicate that long fur is dominant.

C   is incorrect because this would indicate that short fur is dominant.

D   is correct because when a trait displays incomplete dominance, the offspring have a trait that is intermediate to the two phenotypes of the parents.

2. B

A   is incorrect because a recessive allele is not expressed.

B   is correct because allele is defined as one of the alternative forms of a gene.

C   is incorrect because the combination of genes for a specific trait is a definition of a genotype.

D   is incorrect because the complete genetic makeup of a living thing describes a genome, not an allele.

3. A

A   is correct because a gene contains the set of hereditary instructions that determine a specific trait, or detectable characteristic, in a person.

B   is incorrect because a phenotype is an organism's appearance, which is determined by the instructions in the genes.

C   is incorrect because many genes are located on a single chromosome.

D   is incorrect because a characteristic of a person is the product of genetic instructions.

4. C

A   is incorrect because all offspring have the smooth shape, so the smooth shape is a dominant trait.

B   is incorrect because all offspring have the smooth shape, so the wrinkled shape is a recessive trait.

C   is correct because only smooth shape shows up in the offspring. Therefore, smooth shape must be the dominant trait.

D   is incorrect because the offspring do not include any peas with wrinkled seeds. Therefore, wrinkled seeds must be the recessive trait.

5. A

A   is correct because height is an inherited trait, and the children share the trait because it was passed on to all of them from their parents.

B   is incorrect because males and females cannot be identical twins.

C   is incorrect because, even though a healthy diet can help children achieve their maximum height, height is an inherited trait rather than an acquired trait.

D   is incorrect. Although the environment plays a role, inherited genes are the main reason all the children are tall.

Lesson 5 Quiz

1. B   4. A
2. D   5. A
3. C

1. B

A   is incorrect because although one parent has the alleles *BB*, the other is *Bb*.

B   is correct because the parental alleles, which are shown at the top and side of the square, are *BB* and *Bb*.

C   is incorrect because although one parent has the alleles *Bb*, the other is *BB*.

D   is incorrect because although one parent has the alleles *Bb*, the other is *BB*.

2. D

A   is incorrect because an allele is an alternative form of a gene.

B   is incorrect because a carrier is an individual who has an allele for a trait but does not show that allele in their phenotype.

C   is incorrect because a pedigree shows family relationships and gives the actual phenotypes of individuals, but it does not show all the potential combinations of alleles that the offspring could inherit.

D   is correct because a Punnett square shows all of the possible ways that parental alleles may combine in the offspring.

3. C

A is incorrect because all inherited genetic disorders can be passed from parent to child.

B is incorrect because both males and females can be affected by sex-linked disorders.

C is correct because a sex-linked gene is located on a sex chromosome.

D is incorrect because the inheritance of sex-linked disorders can be traced on a pedigree.

4. A

A is correct because a ratio compares two quantities and shows the relationship between them.

B is incorrect because this choice describes a pedigree diagram.

C is incorrect because this choice describes a Punnett square.

D is incorrect because this choice describes probability.

5. A

A is correct because on a typical pedigree, boxes represent males and circles represent females.

B is incorrect because pedigrees can trace dominant or recessive traits within a family.

C is incorrect because on a typical pedigree, a shaded shape means a person does have a specific trait.

D is incorrect because a Punnett square, not a pedigree, shows the possible allele combinations that are possible in a given cross.

Lesson 6 Quiz

1. A   4. B
2. D   5. C
3. D

1. A

A is correct because a mutation in DNA can result in an incorrect amino acid being inserted into a protein, such as in the case of sickle-cell anemia.

B is incorrect because replication is the process by which DNA copies itself. Replication does not cause sickle-cell anemia.

C is incorrect because translation is the process by which RNA directs the synthesis of proteins.

D is incorrect because transcription is the process of transferring information from DNA to messenger RNA.

2. D

A is incorrect because DNA is made from nucleotides. Amino acids make up proteins.

B is incorrect because proteins, not DNA, perform the main functions of cells.

C is incorrect because an enzyme is responsible for speeding up a chemical reaction.

D is correct because DNA is a molecule that forms the basis of heredity.

3. D

A is incorrect because the mutation may take place during DNA replication.

B is incorrect because the mutation can affect the way proteins are made by ribosomes, but it does not stop the process of protein synthesis.

C is incorrect because the mutation can change the DNA within a chromosome, but it cannot change the number of chromosomes.

D is correct because this mutation can change the information that flows from DNA to mRNA. As a result, a different amino acid may be inserted into the protein.

4. B

A is incorrect because transcription, not replication, involves making an RNA template from DNA.

B is correct because replication results in identical copies of a DNA molecule.

C is incorrect because translation, not replication, involves moving mRNA through a ribosome.

D is incorrect because mutations, not replication, result in a change in the number, type, or order of bases in DNA.

5. C

A is incorrect because DNA is a double-stranded molecule. This diagram shows a single-stranded molecule.

B is incorrect because this diagram illustrates a nucleotide.

C is correct because DNA has a spiral shape, known as a double helix, that looks like a twisted ladder.

D is incorrect because this diagram illustrates the shape of a chromosome.

Lesson 7 Quiz

1. A   4. B
2. C   5. D
3. D

1. A

A is correct because biotechnology is the application or use of living things and biological processes.

B is incorrect because biotechnology does not necessarily involve the use of electronic devices; artificial selection, for example, does not require the use of electronic devices.

C is incorrect because biotechnology does not necessarily involve the development of instruments. Artificial selection, for example, does not require the development of new instrumentation.

D is incorrect because this describes cloning, which is just one example of biotechnology.

2. C

A is incorrect because artificial selection acts on different versions of genes that are already present in a population.

B is incorrect because artificial selection is an example of biotechnology.

C is correct because genetic engineering is a direct change of an organism's DNA, but artificial selection is not.

D is incorrect because this describes cloning.

3. D

A is incorrect because this advance would not have the greatest benefit.

B is incorrect because this biotechnological advance would not affect the greatest number of people.

C is incorrect because this biotechnological development would not have the greatest impact.

D is correct because rice is a staple for millions of people around the world. Developing such rice crops would mean more and better food for global populations.

4. B

A is incorrect because cloning produces genetically identical organisms, cells, or pieces of genetic material.

B is correct because new breeds of dogs are produced when humans selectively breed existing types of dogs.

C is incorrect because the genetic materials of the dog breeds are not directly manipulated.

D is incorrect because asexual reproduction is the process by which one parent produces offspring. In this case, two dogs are bred.

5. D

A is incorrect because adding a gene from an organism would not make it genetically identical to the one from which it was derived.

B is incorrect because removing a gene from an organism would not make it genetically identical to the one from which it was derived.

C is incorrect because crossing different plants will result in plants that are not genetically identical.

D is correct because a clone is an organism, cell, or piece of genetic material that is genetically identical to the one from which it was derived.

Lesson 1 Alternative Assessment

Understanding the Cycle: Scrapbooks depict the three stages of the cell cycle, show illustrations of each stages, and describe what occurs during each stage.

An Ode to Mitosis: Poems describe the ways that a multicellular organism appreciates mitosis.

Tracking Mitosis: Notes and sketches describe the videos. The strengths and weaknesses of the videos are presented.

This Just In!: New reports describe a new cell that has just formed, explain how the cell formed (including the three stages of the cell cycle), and identify the cell as a unicellular organism or part of a multicellular organism.

To Be DNA: Monologues describe what happens to DNA before and during mitosis.

Why, Oh Why?: Videos explain the reasons that unicellular organisms go through cell division and the reasons that multicellular organisms go through cell division.

Lesson 2 Alternative Assessment

Terms: Terms are defined in students' own words, and then by using a dictionary definition. Last, a paragraph uses the terms to describe meiosis.

Calculations: Calculations tell how many chromosomes are present in a haploid cell from a squirrel and corn, and how many chromosomes are present in a diploid cell from an alligator.

Details: Venn diagrams or other graphic organizers show how meoisis and mitosis are alike and different.

Illustrations: Sketches illustrates the differences between the final stages of meiosis I and meiosis II.

Analysis: Answers explain why meiosis is important for many living things.

Model: Models show one phase of meiosis, and include cell walls, chromosomes, spindle fibers (if appropriate), and so on.

Lesson 3 Alternative Assessment

Plant Detective: Steps explain how to figure out whether the plant reproduces sexually or asexually.

Parent Clone: Journal entries describe the advantages of being genetically identical to a parent.

Sporific!: Illustrations show the life cycle of a plant that produces spores, and explain in which stage the plant best survives harsh conditions.

Diagram It!: Diagram shows how organisms reproduce by mitosis.

What're the Advantages?: Charts show the advantages of asexual and sexual reproduction.

News Flash!: Reports describe what happens after a giant plant that reproduces by budding is discovered with growing buds.

Plan a Garden: Sketches show plants in a garden that reproduce both sexually and asexually, and describe the conditions in which each plant is most likely to succeed.

Switching Roles: Explanations tell why the plant may be changing types of reproduction from growing new roots to blooming.

Explain It!: Drawings with labels explain fertilization for a person who is learning English.

Lesson 4 Alternative Assessment

Alien Eyes: Answers explain what color the alien's eyes are,

and what alleles the father might have.

DNA's Role: Diagrams or sketches explain DNA's role in determining human traits. Diagrams or sketches include labels and descriptions.

Dominance Differences: Entries summarize Mendel's findings, and include diagrams or illustrations as needed.

Dominance Differences: Charts explain how complete dominance, incomplete dominance, and co-dominance are alike and different.

Type Casting: Posters identify the relationship between genotype and phenotype, and include a catchy way to remember what each term means.

Genes and Traits: Paragraphs explain how one gene can be responsible for many traits, and how many genes can be responsible for one trait.

Lesson 5 Alternative Assessment

R = red flower, r = pink flower

	R	r
r	Rr	rr
r	Rr	Rr

L = long stem, l = short stem

	L	L
l	Ll	Ll
l	Ll	Ll

T = thick stem, t = thin stem

	T	T
T	TT	Tt
t	Tt	tt

O = oval leaf, o = round leaf

	O	O
O	OO	OO
o	Oo	Oo

G = solid green leaf, g = spotted green leaf

	G	g
G	GG	Gg
G	GG	Gg

B = big leaf, b = small leaf

	B	B
B	BB	BB
b	Bb	Bb

Alleles selected and flowers sketched will vary.

Lesson 6 Alternative Assessment

Vocabulary: Answers include a personal definition, a dictionary definition, and three sentences that use the term *DNA* correctly.

Details: The components of DNA are accurately identified and the word *nucleotide* is used.

Illustrations: Illustrations accurately portray a DNA molecule and how it replicates.

Examples: Answers give examples of what can happen when a mutation in a piece of DNA occurs, and explain how mutations can happen.

Analysis: Analysis tells how the components of DNA work together.

Lesson 7 Alternative Assessment

Assess the Impact: Lists show the pros and cons of one application of biotechnology.

Comic Strip: Strips show how humans have changed an animal or plant over time, and show the differences between the modern organism and its ancestors.

Just the Facts: Presentations tell how biotechnology is used in forensics or how transgenic organisms are used in scientific research.

Forensics: Explanations describe the technology behind DNA fingerprinting or other ways forensic scientists use biotechnology to help solve crimes.

Transgenic: Explanations identify a transgenic organism and explain how its genes were modified and for what purpose.

Breeding the Best: Explanations describe an organism that has been bred by humans, explain how it differs from its wild ancestors, and describe the qualities that humans promoted through selective breeding.

Performance-Based Assessment

See Unit 2, Lesson 5

2. Answers may vary. Sample answer: I think the two mixed-color eggs will result in the most colorful offspring.

4. Each cell of the Punnett square should contain the letters *RB. Please see an example of the diagram in the Visual Answers section at the end of this Answer Key.*

5. There will be a 100% chance of blue offspring.

7. There are two possible correct answers depending on which solid colored egg is chosen. If the student chose the blue egg, Punnett square cells from left to right and top to bottom should be *BB, BR, BB, and BR.* If the student chose the red egg, cells from left to right and top to bottom should be *RB, RR, RB, and RR. Please see examples of these diagrams in the Visual Answers section at the end of this Answer Key.*

8. There are two possible correct answers depending on which solid colored egg is chosen. If the student chose the blue egg, 100% of offspring will be blue. If the student chose the red egg, 50% of offspring will be red and 50% will be blue.

9. From left to right and top to bottom, cells should be *BB, BR, RB, and RR. Please see an example of the diagram in the Visual Answers section at the end of this Answer Key.*

10. Sample answer: There is a 25% chance that the offspring will be red. There is a 75% chance that the offspring will be blue.

13. Sample answer: My results support my hypothesis. I predicted that the offspring of the mixed-color eggs would have the most colorful offspring because both colors were present in both eggs. My results were consistent with this because the Punnett square showed that both red and blue offspring from those

two eggs can be expected to be produced.

14. Sample answer: No, you cannot exactly predict offspring traits for individual cases. You can only state the likelihood that a certain combination will occur.

Unit Review

Vocabulary

1. **DNA** See Unit 2, Lesson 6
2. **ratio** See Unit 2, Lesson 5
3. **clone** See Unit 2, Lesson 7
4. **Meiosis** See Unit 2, Lesson 2
5. **asexual** See Unit 2, Lesson 3

Key Concepts

6. D	10. D	14. B
7. A	11. B	15. A
8. C	12. C	16. A
9. D	13. C	17. B

6. **D See Unit 2, Lesson 4**

A is incorrect because sex-linked inheritance does not produce an intermediate phenotype.

B is incorrect because co-dominance would produce mice with both black and white hairs.

C is incorrect because each offspring would have either black fur or white fur.

D is correct because both alleles contribute to the phenotype of a heterozygote in incomplete dominance, producing an intermediate phenotype.

7. **A See Unit 2, Lesson 1**

A is correct because the new cells that form from mitosis are genetically identical to

the parent cells and they replace the damaged cells.

B is incorrect because meiosis occurs only in the reproductive structures of an organism.

C is incorrect because replication produces new molecules of DNA, not new cells.

D is incorrect because transcription transfers genetic information from DNA to mRNA.

8. **C See Unit 2, Lesson 6**

A is incorrect because no bases have been deleted.

B is incorrect because no additional bases have been inserted.

C is correct because adenine (A) has been substituted for cytosine (C) in the third position. Thymine (T) is now paired with the substituted adenine (A). Originally guanine (G) that was at that position.

D is incorrect because transcription is a process, not a kind of mutation.

9. **D See Unit 2, Lesson 2**

A is incorrect because chromosomes in sex cells are needed to transmit genetic information to the next generation.

B is incorrect because homologous chromosomes are chromosome pairs. A sex cell contains only one of each pair.

C is incorrect because sex cells have half the normal number

of chromosomes in the zygote. Fertilization results in a single zygote that has the correct number of chromosomes for a body cell.

D is correct because fertilization and formation of the zygote restores the full set of chromosomes found in body cells.

10. **D See Unit 2, Lesson 2**

A is incorrect because the chromatids do not separate during meiosis I.

B is incorrect because chromatids separate during meiosis II.

C is incorrect because DNA cannot replicate in the middle of meiosis.

D is correct because chromatids remain together during meiosis I and separate during meiosis II.

11. **B See Unit 2, Lesson 6**

A is incorrect because A pairs with T and C pairs with G.

B is correct because this pairing, A with T and C with G, results in equal amounts of A and T, and C and G. This is known as Chargaff's rule.

C is incorrect because the chemical composition of a nucleotide cannot explain the percentage of each base in a DNA sample.

D is incorrect because having the bases on the interior of the DNA molecule cannot explain the percentage of each base.

12. C See Unit 2, Lesson 3

A is incorrect because asexual reproduction occurs quickly.

B is incorrect because only one parent is needed.

C is correct because large numbers of organisms are produced in a relatively short period of time.

D is incorrect because offspring are identical to the parent. No genetic diversity is produced.

13. C See Unit 2, Lesson 4

A is incorrect because co-dominance would produce offspring with mottled blue and white flowers.

B is incorrect because no offspring could have white flowers if blue were recessive.

C is correct because only one allele of the blue flower trait needs to be inherited for the gene to be expressed in the phenotype (so it is dominant). Therefore, each parent must have one allele for blue flowers if the ratio of blue to white flowers in the offspring is 3:1.

D is incorrect because incomplete dominance would cause an intermediate color in *Ff* offspring.

14. B See Unit 2, Lesson 1

A is incorrect because cell division would form two unicellular organisms rather than one larger organism.

B is correct because reproduction is the formation of two organisms from a single parent cell that are genetically identical to the parent.

C is incorrect because unicellular organisms do not produce sex cells.

D is incorrect because cell division would form two unicellular organisms rather than repair any damage to the cell.

15. A See Unit 2, Lesson 3

A is correct because the diploid number is restored by fertilization.

B is incorrect because gametes from two parents are involved in fertilization.

C is incorrect because the zygote would have too many chromosomes.

D is incorrect because the zygote would have only one chromosome of each pair.

16. A See Unit 2, Lesson 1 and Lesson 2

A is correct because the two chromatids of each chromosome have not yet separated in anaphase I. Only homologous pairs separate during meiosis I.

B is incorrect because chromosomes in meiosis I have two chromatids; chromosomes in mitosis have one.

C is incorrect because only the chromosomes can be seen, not DNA itself.

D is incorrect because a sex cell that forms cannot contain both homologous chromosomes.

17. B See Unit 2, Lesson 6

A is incorrect because this is the same sequence as the original strand.

B is correct because a strand of DNA serves as a template by adding complementary bases when a new strand is made during replication.

C is incorrect because uracil is not found in DNA.

D is incorrect because uracil is found only in RNA, not in DNA.

Critical Thinking
18. See Unit 2, Lesson 6

- *The genetic information is transferred in the nucleus from DNA to mRNA during transcription.*

- *mRNA carries the information to rRNA in the ribosome. tRNA brings amino acids to the ribosome, where proteins chains are assembled during translation.*

- *Transcription takes place in the nucleus and translation takes place in the cytoplasm, in the ribosomes.*

19. See Unit 2, Lesson 5

- *Straight hair is controlled by a recessive allele because the offspring of a parent with straight hair and a parent with curly hair will most likely have curly hair.*

- *A recessive trait can appear in an offspring of two parents who do not exhibit the trait.*

- *The trait cannot be sex-linked because both males and females express the straight hair phenotype in equal proportions.*

20. See Unit 2, Lesson 7

- *Biotechnology has advantages and disadvantages.*

- Positive effect: *Mosquitoes can be genetically engineered so they do not spread malaria.*

- Negative effect: *If a gene from a plant that people are allergic to is inserted into a different kind of plant, people could become allergic to that plant.*

Connect Essential Questions

21. See Unit 2, Lesson 4 and Lesson 5

- *The genotype in the first box is* AA. *The genotype in the top right and bottom left boxes is* Aa. *The genotype of the bottom right box is* aa.

- *The phenotype in the first three boxes is free-hanging earlobes. The phenotype of the aa genotype is attached.*

- *Free-hanging earlobes are inherited as a simple dominant trait.*

- *There will be an expected ratio of 3 free-hanging phenotypes to 1 attached earlobes phenotype.*

Unit Test A

Key Concepts

1. D	6. C	11. D
2. C	7. A	12. A
3. B	8. D	13. C
4. A	9. C	14. C
5. D	10. D	15. D

1. D

A is incorrect because the image shows cytokinesis. During mitosis, the nucleus divides, but the cell itself does not divide until cytokinesis

B is incorrect because during anaphase, chromatids separate. This stage occurs before the division of the cell.

C is incorrect because if the image showed interphase, the cell would be undergoing normal life activities and not dividing.

D is correct because the phases of mitosis are complete, and the new cells are undergoing the final division into two daughter cells. This stage of the cell cycle is cytokinesis.

2. C

A is incorrect because only sexual reproduction requires two parents.

B is incorrect because only asexual reproduction results in genetically identical offspring.

C is correct because genetic information is transmitted from parents to offspring, mostly by chromosomes, in both types of reproduction.

D is incorrect because some organisms can reproduce sexually or asexually, but not all organisms have this ability.

3. B

A is incorrect because the kinds of nutrients the plant will need does not pose a risk.

B is correct because there might be unanticipated side effects of genetically engineered plants that could pose a risk to human health.

C is incorrect because whether or not a plant will grow well in different soils is a consideration, but not a risk.

D is incorrect because selecting plants for crossbreeding poses no risk or danger.

4. A

A is correct because spores are specialized cells formed by fungi.

B is incorrect because yeasts do not form as spores.

C is incorrect because plantlets are tiny plants that form along the leaves of some plants.

D is incorrect because the parent fungi are the larger structures in the picture.

5. D

A is incorrect because most multicellular organisms do grow larger.

B is incorrect because cell division, not the growth of individual cells, causes multicellular organisms to grow larger.

C is incorrect because multicellular organisms do not grow larger by acquiring cells from elsewhere.

D is correct because cell division causes multicellular organisms to grow larger.

6. C

A is incorrect because replication is the process by which DNA is copied.

B is incorrect because transcription is the process of transferring information from DNA to mRNA.

C is correct because translation is the process by which RNA directs the formation of proteins.

D is incorrect because this is just one part of translation.

7. A

A is correct because an extra base has been inserted into the original DNA sequence.

B is incorrect because a different base pair has replaced the original one, resulting in a mutation called a substitution.

C is incorrect because a base has been left out of the new DNA sequence. This type of mutation is called a deletion.

D is incorrect because the new DNA sequence matches the original DNA sequence, meaning that no mutation has taken place.

8. D

A is incorrect because, as carriers, Alisha and Rob each have an allele for the disease, but they are not immune to the disease.

B is incorrect because Alisha and Rob are carriers of the disease, but they will not develop the disease. To be expressed, the disease requires two alleles.

C is incorrect because as carriers of the disease, Alisha and Rob do not have the disease. To be expressed, the disease requires two alleles.

D is correct because each parent, as a carrier of the disease, has one allele for the disease. Neither has the disease because, to be expressed, the disease requires two alleles. Each or both parent could pass the allele to a child.

9. C

A is incorrect because acquired traits are due to environmental factors, not inherited factors.

B is correct because a phenotype is an observable trait; environmental factors and not phenotypes are responsible for acquired traits.

C is correct because acquired traits, such as skills, are due to environmental factors.

D is incorrect because acquired traits are due to environmental factors, not genetic material.

10. D

A is incorrect because cloning is a laboratory procedure that yields genetically identical organisms, cells, or pieces of genetic information; clones do not result from selective breeding.

B is incorrect because biologically similar organisms are not always genetically identical.

C is incorrect because artificially selected organisms are generally those chosen for breeding purposes to produce new traits, not to produce genetically identical organisms.

D is correct because clones are genetically identical organisms.

11. D

A is incorrect because codominance takes place when the two different alleles for a trait are both expressed.

B is incorrect because the word nondominance is not used to describe a trait. A trait can be dominant, recessive, or codominant, or it can exhibit incomplete dominance.

C is incorrect because if the trait for flower color were an example of complete dominance, the offspring would have either red or white flowers.

D is correct because having a trait that is intermediate to the phenotypes of both parents is an example of incomplete dominance.

12. A

A is correct because this box represents the possibility of each parent passing an A allele on to the offspring.

B is incorrect because *Aa* should appear only in boxes representing offspring that inherited an *A* allele from one parent and an *a* allele from the other parent.

C is incorrect because *aa* should appear only in boxes representing offspring that inherited an *a* allele from both parents.

D is incorrect because there is enough information to know that the offspring would be *AA*.

13. C

A is incorrect because anaphase is the third phase of mitosis.

B is incorrect because telophase is the last phase of mitosis.

C is correct because prophase is the first phase of mitosis.

D is incorrect because metaphase is the second phase of mitosis.

14. C

A is incorrect because this statement describes binary fission.

B is incorrect because this statement describes spore formation.

C is correct because vegetative reproduction takes place when new plants develop from modified stems or roots of the parent plant.

D is incorrect because this statement describes sexual reproduction.

15. D

A is incorrect because the offspring will inherit half of their chromosomes from each parent.

B is incorrect because this diploid cell has 8 chromosomes, so sex cells will receive 4 chromosomes.

C is incorrect because the offspring will inherit one chromosome from each pair.

D is correct because the offspring will inherit half of the total chromosomes, one from each homologous pair.

Critical Thinking
16.

• meiosis

• description of meiosis (*e.g., Meiosis is cell division involved in sexual reproduction. Meiosis takes place only in reproductive structures. During meiosis, sex cells are created in an organism's reproductive structures. The new sex cells have half the number of chromosomes as body cells. The original number of chromosomes are restored during the fertilization of the cells during reproduction*; etc.)

Extended Response
17.

• one parent: *GG*

• other parent: *gg*

• *GG* parent: always pass a *G* allele to offspring

• *gg* parent: always pass a *g* allele to offspring

Unit Test B
Key Concepts
1. B   6. D   11. C
2. B   7. D   12. C
3. A   8. B   13. C
4. C   9. D   14. B
5. C   10. A   15. B

1. B

A is incorrect because the image shows cytokinesis. The two stages that happen before are interphase and mitosis.

B is correct because the image shows cytokinesis. The two stages that happen before cytokinesis are interphase and mitosis.

C is incorrect because the image shows cytokinesis. Interphase and mitosis happen before cytokinesis.

D is incorrect because the image shows cytokinesis. Interphase and mitosis happen before cytokinesis.

2. B

A is incorrect because organisms that reproduce asexually are less likely to expend energy to find a mate.

B is correct because the offspring of asexual reproduction typically do not require additional effort or care.

C is incorrect because asexual reproduction requires only one parent.

D is incorrect because organisms that reproduce asexually are less likely to have offspring genetically different from themselves.

3. A

A is correct because greater availability of oranges as a food source would benefit society.

B is incorrect because reduced orange crop yield would not be a benefit to society.

C is incorrect because an increased cost of oranges would not be a benefit to society.

D is incorrect because it is not clear whether a change in the distribution of insects that pollinate orange flowers would have a positive, neutral, or negative effect on society.

4. C

A is incorrect because budding occurs when an organism develops tiny buds on its body to form a new organism. The diagram shows spores being released.

B is incorrect because binary fission occurs when an organism splits into two identical organisms. The diagram shows spores being released.

C is correct because these fungi are reproducing by spore formation. The diagram shows spores being released from fungi.

D is incorrect because vegetative reproduction involves the production of new plants growing from the stems, roots, or leaves of existing plants. The diagram shows spores being released from fungi.

5. C

A is incorrect because though multicellular organisms develop specialized cells, this doesn't explain the process by which damaged cells are replaced.

B is incorrect because cells don't grow larger to replace damaged cells; they divide. The new, healthy cells replace injured or damaged cells.

C is correct because damaged cells are replaced with new cells when healthy cells divide; this process helps keep organisms healthy.

D is incorrect because healthy cells divide and work to replace damaged cells.

6. D

A is incorrect because DNA does not exit the cytoplasm during translation.

B is incorrect because the mutation should not affect the ability of amino acids to come to the ribosome during translation. The mutation only results in a change of the sequence of bases that will be translated.

C is incorrect because mutations change DNA, not the shape of amino acids.

D is correct because a deletion mutation will change the sequence of bases that will be transcribed to form proteins.

7. D

A is incorrect because a deletion mutation takes place when a nucleotide base is left out of the DNA molecule.

B is incorrect because an insertion mutation takes place when a nucleotide base is added to the original DNA sequence.

C is incorrect because translation is the process by which the mRNA strand directs the synthesis of proteins.

D is correct because a substitution mutation takes place when a different base pair is inserted into a DNA molecule.

8. B

A is incorrect because the allele for color blindness is on the X chromosome, and males inherit only a Y chromosome from their fathers.

B is correct because the allele for color blindness is on the X chromosome. Males inherit a single X chromosome, and it is inherited from their mother.

C is incorrect because the man will not pass on the allele for color blindness to his sons. He will pass on a Y chromosome to his sons, and the allele for color blindness is on the X chromosome.

D is incorrect because males only inherit a single X chromosome, so they have only one allele for the color blindness trait.

9. D

A is incorrect because eye color is an inherited trait.

B is incorrect because hair color is an inherited trait.

C is incorrect because blood type is an inherited trait.

D is correct because table manners are acquired, or learned, traits.

10. A

A   is correct because clones are organisms that are genetically identical.

B   is incorrect because mutation changes DNA, and these mice have the same DNA.

C   is incorrect because selection cannot account for the production of genetically identical mice.

D   is incorrect because isolation does not describe a process for producing genetically identical mice.

11. C

A   is incorrect because both alleles are not expressed. Therefore, this is not an example of codominance.

B   is incorrect because asexual reproduction involves one parent, not two.

C   is correct because when both alleles are present, only the dominant allele for blue flower color is expressed.

D   is incorrect because the dominant allele masks the recessive allele, so the scenario is an example of complete dominance.

12. C

A   is incorrect because a cross between these parents would produce offspring in a ratio of 1 *DD* to 1 *Dd*.

B   is incorrect because a cross between these parents would produce offspring in a ratio of 1 *DD* to 2 *Dd* to 1 *dd*.

C   is correct because a cross between these parents would

produce offspring in a ratio of 1 *Dd* to 1 *dd*.

D   is incorrect because a cross between these parents would produce only offspring with *Dd*.

13. C

A   is incorrect because during anaphase, the cell would not have two nuclei.

B   is incorrect because during prophase, the cell would have one nucleus.

C   is correct because chromosomes are still visible and the cell has two nuclei during telophase, the last stage of mitosis; the nuclear membrane forms around what will be each new nucleus.

D   is incorrect because during interphase, the genetic material would be in the form of chromatin, not visible chromosomes, and the cell would not have two nuclei.

14. B

A   is incorrect because fertilization is required for sexual reproduction.

B   is correct because all three of these modes of reproduction are asexual.

C   is incorrect because fertilization is required for sexual reproduction.

D   is incorrect because egg and sperm join in fertilization as part of sexual reproduction.

15. B

A   is incorrect because chromosomes are duplicated

during both meiosis and mitosis.

B   is correct because homologous chromosomes do not pair up during mitosis. This is a feature that is unique to meiosis and is shown in the above image.

C   is incorrect because chromosomes line up along the equatorial plate during both types of cell division; also, such alignment is not shown in the above image.

D   is incorrect because the condensation of chromosomes happens before both meiosis and mitosis.

Critical Thinking
16.

• sex cells created in reproductive structures of an organism

• sex cells: half the number of chromosomes as body cells

• fertilization of cell during reproduction, original number of chromosomes restored

Extended Response
17.

• one parent: *GG*

• other parent: *gg*

• *GG* parent: always pass a *G* allele to offspring

• *gg* parent: always pass a *g* allele to offspring

• other combos (like *Gg*) unlikely

• low probability of other combos; all 1,000 offspring have *Gg* alleles

- if other parent allele combos: likelihood of other offspring combos goes up

End-of-Module Test

1. B	11. B	21. C
2. B	12. D	22. C
3. D	13. B	23. A
4. C	14. A	24. C
5. C	15. B	25. B
6. A	16. D	26. B
7. C	17. D	27. C
8. C	18. A	28. D
9. C	19. D	29. D
10. C	20. C	30. D

1. B See Unit 1, Lesson 5

A in incorrect because a tree losing its leaves is not a behavior; it is an automatic response to changes in the seasons.

B is correct because an animal that hibernates changes its behavior in response to changes in the seasons.

C is incorrect because a human shivering is an involuntary physical response to cold, and doesn't represent a behavior.

D is incorrect because organisms do change their behavior in order to maintain homeostasis; for example, a bear hibernates through the winter.

2. B See Unit 2, Lesson 6

A is incorrect because only messenger RNA (mRNA) participates in transcription.

B is correct because this is describes transcription and translation, and all three kinds of RNA are involved in transcription and translation.

C is incorrect because ribosomal RNA (rRNA) is the only RNA that forms a part of ribosomes, where amino acid chains are assembled.

D is incorrect because only transfer RNA (tRNA) delivers amino acids to a ribosome.

3. D See Unit 2, Lesson 6

A is incorrect because Francis Crick was one of the co-discoverers of the double-helix structure of DNA, which is point 6 in the timeline.

B is incorrect because James Watson was one of the co-discoverers of the structure of the DNA molecule, at point 6 in the timeline.

C is incorrect because Erwin Chargaff discovered the rules by which the nucleotide bases in DNA form pairs; his name belongs at point 4 in the timeline.

D is correct because Rosalind Franklin used x-ray diffraction to make images of the shape of DNA, which is point 5 in the timeline.

4. C See Unit 2, Lesson 4

A is incorrect because the alleles are codominant, so both phenotypes are expressed.

B is incorrect because both alleles contribute to the phenotype in order to produce blood type AB.

C is correct because both alleles contribute to the phenotype in

order to produce blood type AB.

A is incorrect because individuals with blood type AB produce antigens associated with type A and type B blood.

5. C See Unit 1, Lesson 1

A is incorrect because DNA is contained within most cells and is necessary for cell division, one of the many necessary life processes.

B is incorrect because organelles are structures contained within most cells that help the cell to perform life processes.

C is correct because an organism is made up of one or more cells and carries out all of its own activities for life.

D is incorrect because cytoplasm is the region inside the cell membrane that includes the fluid and all of the organelles except the nucleus.

6. A See Unit 2, Lesson 4

A is correct because the wrinkled shape is recessive, which is why the trait is not observed in the offspring.

B is incorrect because the round shape, not the wrinkled shape, is the dominant trait.

C is incorrect because an acquired trait is not inherited.

D is incorrect because all the offspring show a trait possessed by one of the parent plants and not some combination of traits from both parent plants.

7. C See Unit 2, Lesson 7

A is incorrect because removing algae may affect food chains.

B is incorrect because a fertilizer may pollute the environment.

C is correct because treating wastewater with microbes can remove pollutants that could negatively affect the environment.

D is incorrect because eliminating pet odors may be nice for people, but it is not the most beneficial use of biotechnology for the environment.

8. C See Unit 2, Lesson 1

A is incorrect because ants are multicellular organisms that rely on mitosis for growth and repair but not for reproduction.

B is incorrect because bluebirds are multicellular organisms that rely on mitosis for growth and repair but not for reproduction.

C is correct because single-celled eukaryotes reproduce through mitosis.

D is incorrect because jellyfish are multicellular organisms that rely on mitosis for growth and repair but not for reproduction.

9. C See Unit 1, Lesson 6

A is incorrect because light energy comes from the sun. Plants use light energy for photosynthesis.

B is incorrect because kinetic energy is the energy of an object in motion.

C is correct because the energy stored in food is in the chemical bonds of molecules of food that are broken down when energy is needed.

D is incorrect because mechanical energy relates to the amount of work an object can do, not to energy stored in food.

10. C See Unit 1, Lesson 3

A is incorrect because cellular respiration takes place in the mitochondria.

B is incorrect because cellular respiration does not produce proteins and happens in cells almost all of the time.

C is correct because cellular respiration breaks down sugars to release the energy stored in sugar.

D is incorrect because it takes place in the mitochondria, which do have a membrane.

11. B See Unit 2, Lesson 3

A is incorrect because the image shows sexual reproduction. Cell A and Cell B are combining in the process of fertilization.

B is correct because the image shows Cell A and Cell B combining in the process of fertilization, which is part of sexual reproduction. After fertilization, a zygote with a full set of chromosomes is formed.

C is incorrect because binary fission, a type of asexual reproduction, occurs when a parent organism splits into two genetically-identical

organisms. The image shows fertilization.

D is incorrect because the image shows sexual reproduction, not asexual reproduction.

12. D See Unit 2, Lesson 2

A is incorrect because one round of mitosis would result in only two identical daughter cells, each with a complete set of chromosomes.

B is incorrect because two rounds of mitosis would result in four identical daughter cells, each with a complete set of chromosomes.

C is incorrect because the drawing shows meiosis I followed by meiosis II, where the sister chromatids separate.

D is correct because four sex cells are produced, each with half the original number of chromosomes.

13. B See Unit 1, Lesson 3

A is incorrect because nuclei are found inside cells.

B is correct because a cell membrane surrounds all cells, and a cell wall surrounds the cell membrane in plant cells, fungal cells, and bacterial cells.

C is incorrect because both the cytoplasm and the cytoskeleton are found within cells.

D is incorrect because the cytoplasm is found within cells.

14. A See Unit 2, Lesson 4

A is correct because the plant could display the trait of a tall stem or a dwarf stem. The environmental conditions, such as water and sunlight, would also have a major influence.

B is incorrect because the plant's genes and the environment would both be major influences.

C is incorrect because the genes would also have a major influence on the height of the plant.

D is incorrect because the environment would also have a major influence on the height of the plant.

15. B See Unit 1, Lesson 6

A is incorrect because ATP is a product of cellular respiration, not a starting material, and carbon dioxide is a waste product, not energy.

B is correct because cellular respiration uses oxygen to break down food in the form of glucose and releases energy in the form of ATP.

C is incorrect because hydrogen is not a starting material of cellular respiration.

D is incorrect because carbon dioxide is a product of the cellular respiration process, not a starting material.

16. D See Unit 2, Lesson 3

A is incorrect because changing environmental conditions is a reason why sexual reproduction is advantageous,

but it does not best explain the purpose of reproduction.

B is incorrect because complex body structures are a characteristic of sexual reproduction. It does not explain why reproduction in general in necessary.

C is incorrect because sexual reproduction increases genetic variability, but not all organisms reproduce sexually, so this is not the best answer.

D is correct because reproduction is the mechanism by which parents pass on their genetic material. Without reproduction, a species would die out.

17. D See Unit 2, Lesson 2

A is incorrect because an egg is a sex cell, which is a product of meiosis.

B is incorrect because a sperm is a sex cell, which is a product of meiosis.

C is incorrect because a sex cell is a product of meiosis.

D is correct because mitosis produces body cells, such as skin cells and brain cells.

18. A See Unit 1, Lesson 2

A is correct because water is a molecule made up of hydrogen and oxygen atoms held together by chemical bonds. Water is also a compound because it is made up of two elements. Compounds are made up of two or more elements.

B is incorrect because oxygen gas is a molecule made up of

oxygen atoms held together by chemical bonds. Oxygen is not a compound because it is only made up of one element. Compounds are made up of two or more elements.

C is incorrect because oxygen is not a compound because it is only made up of one element. Compounds are made up of two or more elements.

D is incorrect because water is a compound because it is made up of two elements. Compounds are made up of two or more elements.

19. D See Unit 1, Lesson 1

A is incorrect because an organelle is a structure inside a cell and is not a type of cell.

B is incorrect because a membrane is a structure that surrounds a cell and is not a type of cell.

C is incorrect because a eukaryotic cell has a nucleus, and this cell does not have a nucleus.

D is correct because a prokaryotic cell has no nucleus, but contains its DNA in the cytoplasm.

20. C See Unit 2, Lesson 5

A is incorrect because both males and females can have sex-linked genes.

B is incorrect because both males and females can have sex-linked genes.

C is correct because a sex-linked gene is a gene that is located on a sex chromosome.

D is incorrect because sex-linked genes do not cause sexually transmitted disease, they are caused by viruses, bacteria, and other pathogens.

21. C See Unit 1, Lesson 5

A is incorrect because cellular respiration does not produce sugars.

B is incorrect because cellular respiration, not photosynthesis, requires oxygen. Also, photosynthesis, not cellular respiration, requires carbon dioxide.

C is correct because photosynthesis produces oxygen, and cellular respiration produces carbon dioxide.

D is incorrect because cellular respiration, not photosynthesis, requires energy from food and photosynthesis, not cellular respiration, requires energy from the sun.

22. C See Unit 1, Lesson 4

A is incorrect because an organ is part of an organ system, which makes up an organism.

B is incorrect because tissues make up organs, which can be part of an organ system.

C is correct because the animal's body, or the organism, is the most specialized level of organization. The animal's body is made up of tissues, organs, and organ systems.

D is incorrect because an organ system is part of an organism.

23. A See Unit 1, Lesson 3

A is correct because the presence of a nucleus is a characteristic of eukaryotic cells and is not found in prokaryotic cells.

B is incorrect because cytoplasm is found in both prokaryotic and eukaryotic cells.

C is incorrect because a cell membrane is found in both prokaryotic and eukaryotic cells.

D is incorrect because genetic material is found in both prokaryotic and eukaryotic cells.

24. C See Unit 2, Lesson 2

A is incorrect because meiosis takes place in reproductive organs, and a bone is not a reproductive organ.

B is incorrect because mitosis produces body cells, and not mature sex cells, which are made in the testes.

C is correct because meiosis takes place in reproductive organs such as the ovaries.

D is incorrect because meiosis takes place in reproductive organs, and the stomach is not a reproductive organ.

25. B See Unit 2, Lesson 7

A is incorrect because cloning creates a genetic duplicate.

B is correct because a donkey and horse are deliberately chosen for mating purposes.

C is incorrect because genetic engineering involves modifying the hereditary material.

D is incorrect because cell and tissue cultures are used to grow cells and tissues in a laboratory.

26. B See Unit 2, Lesson 1

A is incorrect because mitosis is another part of the cell cycle, which includes interphase and cytokinesis.

B is correct because the cell cycle includes interphase, mitosis, and cytokinesis.

C is incorrect because cytokinesis is another part of the cell cycle, which includes interphase and mitosis.

D is incorrect because although cell division is involved in reproduction, interphase is not a stage of reproduction.

27. C See Unit 2, Lesson 5

A is incorrect because the Punnett square predicts an equal ratio of 2:2 or 1:1 offspring.

B is incorrect because this choice shows that the Punnett square predicts only *BB* offspring.

C is correct because the Punnett square predicts equal numbers of *BB* and *Bb* offspring.

D is incorrect because this choice shows that the Punnett square predicts twice as many *Bb* offspring as *BB* offspring. However, the expected ratio is 2:2 or 1:1.

28. D See Unit 1, Lesson 2

A is incorrect because although cells can burst when too much water from outside the cell moves into it, the cell tries to remain balanced. So when the inside of the cell has a higher concentration than the outside of the cell, the water will move out of the cell.

B is incorrect because water moves into a cell from outside the cell only when the concentration of water outside the cell is higher than the concentration of water inside the cell.

C is incorrect because the cell will not remain unchanged, it will attempt to gain a balance. It does this by allowing water to move in or out of the cell.

D is correct because water will move out of the cell when the concentration of water within a cell is higher than the

concentration of water outside the cell.

29. D See Unit 1, Lesson 4

A is incorrect because roots can be of various lengths, and the length of roots is not a function of roots.

B is incorrect because although the roots are connected to the stem, this does not describe what roots do in the plant.

C is incorrect because having root hairs helps the roots function, but the presence of root hairs does not describe a function of roots.

D is correct because taking in nutrients is one of the functions of roots.

30. D See Unit 1, Lesson 5

A is incorrect because the nucleus is within the cell, so materials transported out of the nucleus would still be inside the cell.

B is incorrect because photosynthesis takes place in the chloroplast.

C is incorrect because chromosomes are not involved in materials exchange.

D is correct because the materials are transported into and out of the cell through the semi-permeable cell membrane.

Visual Answers

Unit 2, Performance-Based Assessment, Item 4

	B	B
R	RB	RB
R	RB	RB

Unit 2, Performance-Based Assessment, Item 9

	B	R
B	BB	BR
R	RB	RR

Unit 2, Performance-Based Assessment, Item 7

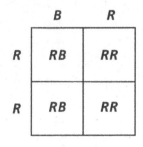
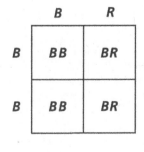

	B	R
R	RB	RR
R	RB	RR

	B	R
B	BB	BR
B	BB	BR